NEW DIRECTIONS FOR ADULT AND CONTINUING EDUCATION

Ralph G. Brockett, *University of Tennessee, Knoxville*
Susan Imel, *Ohio State University*
EDITORS-IN-CHIEF

Alan B. Knox, *University of Wisconsin, Madison*
CONSULTING EDITOR

Mentoring: New Strategies and Challenges

Michael W. Galbraith
Florida Atlantic University

Norman H. Cohen
Community College of Philadelphia

EDITORS

Number 66, Summer 1995

JOSSEY-BASS PUBLISHERS
San Francisco

MENTORING: NEW STRATEGIES AND CHALLENGES
Michael W. Galbraith, Norman H. Cohen (eds.)
New Directions for Adult and Continuing Education, no. 66
Ralph G. Brockett, Susan Imel, Editors-in-Chief
Alan B. Knox, Consulting Editor

Microfilm copies of issues and articles are available in 16mm and 35mm, as well as microfiche in 105mm, through University Microfilms Inc., 300 North Zeeb Road, Ann Arbor, Michigan 48106-1346.

LC 85-644750   ISSN 1052-2891   ISBN 0-7879-9912-1

NEW DIRECTIONS FOR ADULT AND CONTINUING EDUCATION is part of The Jossey-Bass Higher and Adult Education Series and is published quarterly by Jossey-Bass Inc., Publishers, 350 Sansome Street, San Francisco, California 94104-1342. Second-class postage paid at San Francisco, California, and at additional mailing offices. POSTMASTER: Send address changes to New Directions for Adult and Continuing Education, Jossey-Bass Inc., Publishers, 350 Sansome Street, San Francisco, California 94104-1342.

SUBSCRIPTIONS for 1995 cost $48.00 for individuals and $64.00 for institutions, agencies, and libraries.

EDITORIAL CORRESPONDENCE should be sent to the Editor-in-Chief, Ralph G. Brockett, Department of Educational Leadership, University of Tennessee, 239 Claxton Addition, Knoxville, Tennessee 37996-3400.

Cover photograph by Wernher Krutein/PHOTOVAULT © 1990.

CONTENTS

Editors' Notes

Mentoring is not a new phenomenon. It is an age-old idea that still has relevance and meaning in today's world of education, work, and personal development. Our word *mentor* goes all the way back to Homer's *Odyssey*. Odysseus, preparing to begin his epic voyage, entrusts his son, Telemachus, to his friend Mentor, who is to guide Telemachus in the passage from boyhood to manhood. Mentor is an Ithacan elder whom Athena, the Greek goddess of war, wisdom, and craft, has chosen as her vessel so that she herself can oversee Telemachus's upbringing. When Athena speaks through him, Mentor possesses the goddess's glorious qualities. Therefore, as he mentors Odysseus's son, he is wisdom personified. In addition, "he is a classic transitional figure, helping the youth achieve his manhood and confirm his identity in an adult world" (Daloz, 1886, p. 19).

Mentoring is still considered to be a process that advocates for us and assists and guides us through the transitional phases of our adulthood and, in doing so, influences our personal and professional growth and development. In addition, it is linked to the formation of our identity.

Mentoring has received much new attention over the last fifteen years. Wunsch (1994) notes that "from 1980 to 1990, over 380 articles appeared in the popular press and academic journals on mentoring in business and education" (p. 1). Considering all the other disciplines, such as sociology, social work, counseling, psychology, library science, and nursing, that investigate the process of mentoring, we can conclude that much focus has been directed toward the practice of and the research on mentoring.

Mentoring has been investigated in public education, in which the focus has been on both teacher and student development. It has been discussed in relation to its possible role in higher education of enriching student personnel and development functions and of improving the instructional process, student and faculty relations, professional enhancement, and faculty development.

Understanding the growth and development of men and women through the mentoring processes has also been an enduring focus. The function of mentoring in the career development of women in organizations, enhancing their job levels, power, and influence, has been the subject of numerous publications as has the process of mentorship in relation to many individuals' organizational and career development, leadership potential, and learning within business and industry, libraries, and health-related settings.

Although, mentoring has been a popular topic, it has generated much controversy concerning its practice and research validity (Carmin, 1988; Cohen, 1995; Healy and Welchert, 1990; Jacobi, 1991). One purpose of this volume is to describe and clarify various elements of the mentoring process. Another intention is to enhance the reader's understanding of the utility, practice application, and research potential of mentoring in adult and continuing education. The final purpose is to raise important questions and issues that need additional attention if the conceptual and practical dimensions of mentoring are to be advanced. The authors bring a mixture of practical and research experience that can help professionals in education and other fields understand this process called mentoring from a new perspective.

In Chapter One, we examine mentoring in the learning society and the specific opportunities it extends to adult learners for significant personal, academic, and career development. Further, we suggest how mentoring can assist individuals to adapt to a changing society. Besides discussing issues of equity, the chapter also provides new insights and utility for mentoring within the workplace.

Norman H. Cohen, in Chapter Two, presents the Principles of Adult Mentoring Scale, a self-assessment instrument that allows individuals to determine their effectiveness as mentors. The scale provides both scholars and mentor practitioners with a baseline source that allows them to document, analyze, understand, and improve their professional mentoring practice. In addition, guidelines are included to assist those responsible for the design and operation of continuing education programs for mentors.

Kenneth M. Kerr, Donald R. Schulze, and Lyle E. Woodward, in Chapter Three, examine the factors in designing an organizationally sponsored mentoring program and the steps associated with program implementation, such as selecting a director, selecting mentors and protégés, conducting an orientation, matching mentors and protégés, providing follow-up activities, and engaging in program assessment. In addition, the authors recommend several items to be considered in appraising a new or ongoing mentoring program.

In Chapter Four, Amy W. Johnson and Judith A. Sullivan discuss the design and effectiveness of mentoring programs for at-risk young adults. They use insights gained from their association with the Sponsor-A-Scholar program to present an in-depth analysis of a model mentoring program and to provide useful information on program evaluation. Johnson and Sullivan raise an interesting notion concerning the role adult and continuing educators may play in assisting transitioning young adults into adulthood.

Susan F. Schulz, in Chapter Five, describes the developmental benefits of mentoring, examining the benefits a mentoring relationship may have on the mentor, the mentee, the organization, and the society. Schulz provides illustrations and examples that can help educators and others recognize the power and potential of mentoring.

In Chapter Six, Yvonne Enid Gonzalez Rodriguez explores the issue of diversity as it relates to mentoring in a multicultural society. She raises important questions regarding the intent and outcomes of mentoring culturally diverse individuals who find themselves in predominantly white settings. Strategies for mentoring to diversity are also examined.

Linda Marie Golian, in Chapter Seven, presents various strategies and resources for individuals interested in mentoring. She suggests that engaging in professional development opportunities is essential to cultivating productive mentoring alliances. The last half of Chapter Seven comprises an anno- tated bibliography of important and relevant books, book chapters, journal articles, and workbooks on the process of mentoring.

In Chapter Eight, we describe some of the issues and challenges con- fronting the practice and research of mentoring. We conclude by suggesting that good mentoring can extend lifelong learning opportunities in the com- munity of learners and that good instruction has a foundation in the identified functions of mentoring.

Mentoring: New Strategies and Challenges has been written and compiled to further the understanding of mentoring. We hope it enhances the dialogue concerning mentoring and generates new perspectives concerning adult and continuing education and mentoring.

Michael W. Galbraith
Norman H. Cohen
Editors

References

Carmin, C. N. "Issues in Research on Mentoring: Definitional and Methodological." *Inter- national Journal of Mentoring*, 1988, 2, 9–13.

Cohen, N. H. *Mentoring Adult Learners: A Guide for Educators and Trainers.* Malabar, Fla.: Krieger, 1995.

Daloz, L. A. *Effective Teaching and Mentoring: Realizing the Transformational Power of Adult Learning Experiences.* San Francisco: Jossey-Bass, 1986.

Healy, C. C., and Welchert, A. J. "Mentoring Relations: A Definition to Advance Research and Practice." *Educational Researcher,* 1990, 19 (9), 17–21.

Jacobi, M. "Mentoring and Undergraduate Academic Success: A Literature Review." *Review of Educational Research,* 1991, 61 (4), 505–532.

Wunsch, M. A. "Editor's Notes." In M. A. Wunsch (ed.), *Mentoring Revisited: Making an Impact on Individuals and Institutions.* New Directions for Teaching and Learning, no. 57. San Francisco: Jossey-Bass, 1994.

MICHAEL W. GALBRAITH *is professor of adult education in the Department of Educa- tional Leadership at Florida Atlantic University in Boca Raton and currently serves as editor-in-chief of the national book series* Professional Practices in Adult Edu- cation and Human Resource Development.

NORMAN H. COHEN *is associate professor of English at Community College of Phila- delphia. He holds a doctorate in adult education and is actively involved in the study of mentoring theory and practice and in the application of the mentoring model of learning to education, business, and government. He is author of* Mentoring Adult Learners: A Guide for Educators and Trainers.

The mentoring model of one-to-one interaction is an important approach to lifelong learning and a pragmatic method of helping diverse citizens to adapt to rapidly changing personal, social, and workplace situations.

Mentoring in the Learning Society

Norman H. Cohen, Michael W. Galbraith

Mentoring offers adult learners opportunities for significant personal, academic, and career development. Mentor-mentee relationships provide unique learning experiences because mentees can explore and expand their talents in the company of concerned professionals who have chosen the role of mentor. Mentoring is a pragmatic approach that helps mentees to successfully navigate the complex and rapid social and economic transitions that characterize our century.

Sponsored mentoring programs are planned interventions that organize the mentor-mentee matches and focus the mutual commitment of the participants on creating relationships that are initiated to maximize the learning of mentees. As advocates, mentors are sources of considerable influence who directly attempt to assist their mentees in benefiting from the great variety of educational, training, and employment possibilities available in our society. Mentoring is therefore a deliberate effort to support traditional and nontraditional students from diverse backgrounds in formal and informal settings. The one-to-one mentoring model is very much in harmony with the lifelong learning philosophy of adult and continuing education (Cohen, 1995).

The Mentoring Model of Learning

Mentoring is a one-to-one interactive process of guided developmental learning based on the premise that the participants will have reasonably frequent contact and sufficient interactive time together. Mentors contribute their knowledge, proficiency, and experience to assist mentees who are working toward the achievement of their own objectives. As the relationship evolves, mentees usually interpret the collaborative learning experience with and from their mentors as increasingly important to them.

New Directions for Adult and Continuing Education, no. 66, Summer 1995   © Jossey-Bass Inc., Publishers

What Mentors Offer. Mentors provide a blend of assistance to promote the development of mentees. The complete mentor role has been defined as comprising six separate but interrelated functions: relationship emphasis, information emphasis, facilitative focus, confrontive focus, mentor model, and mentee vision (see Chapter Two). As a highly significant influence, the competent mentor demonstrates skills by effectively interacting with the mentee to support and advance learning, whether that learning is associated with educational or career goals.

Usually, mentee learning is characterized by progressive development, though the charged power of a single dialogue or event sometimes can be of major importance. Generally, mentors gradually establish a collaborative and evolving relationship with mentees for the purpose of enabling them to take appropriate risks, deal better with stress and uncertainty, develop more self-confidence, make more informed decisions, and attain immediate and future objectives. To provide this enriched assistance, mentors function as positive and active role models in the lives of their mentees.

What Mentees Receive. The image of the journey is frequently used to portray the mentor-mentee experience. It is a useful metaphor because the mentee as learner is considered to be on a journey of self-development while the mentor is viewed as the wise teacher who accompanies, encourages, instructs, challenges, and even confronts the mentee as the mentee is faced with making decisions and taking actions. Thus, while on the one hand mentees are perceived as unique individuals, on the other hand they are all viewed as inexperienced persons on personal journeys in the company of experienced persons. Mentees do not explore the world in isolation; they travel with mentors who are recognized as highly important resources on the voyage (Daloz, 1986).

The mentor serves as observer, commentator, and advocate—as influential presence. From mentors, mentees receive specific guidance about the path ahead as well as direct feedback about how they are currently performing on their specific journey. For mentees truly to benefit from the help offered by a mentoring relationship, they need mentor participation that is based on mutual trust; accurate and reliable information; realistic exploration of their goals, decisions, and options; challenges to their ideas, beliefs, and actions; holistic support (intellectual, psychological, emotional) of their efforts; and encouragement to pursue their dreams.

Mentoring and Adaptation to Change

Individuals who believe they have minimal influence over their own destiny often retreat into passive noninvolvement. Some even succumb as casualties to forces within the culture that appear to overwhelm and paralyze them. As guided learning, mentoring helps adult learners deal personally with real-world problems and actively seek relevant solutions because it provides them with the constructive feedback they need to develop more effective adaptive responses. A clear goal of the one-to-one model of learning is to assist citizens to anticipate and actively prepare for inevitable change and to energize them into more positive and competent participation as decision makers in a lifelong learning society (Galbraith, 1991).

Of course, since no single response can be the solution to the increasing demands of accelerating change in our culture, a multifaceted approach to learning is required. The mentoring experience is viewed as one of the important facets because it enables citizens not only to cope with change but also to become proactive beneficiaries of change. Mentoring is an overt attempt to counteract our society's waste of human resources, a tragic personal as well as national loss of fulfillment and talent.

The practical goals of mentoring therefore involve more than a series of reactive lessons in survival, prevention of the loss of ability, or recovery of resources. Mentor-mentee involvement is a powerful opportunity for genuine enrichment of intellectual and affective capacities. When conducted by professionals who understand adult learners and perform as skilled practitioners of interpersonal communication, mentoring can be a pivotal educational event because it teaches adults to function more effectively as independent problem solvers and self-generating continuing learners (Brookfield, 1991).

In our contemporary society, there are many benefits offered by mentoring that are relevant to a large population of adult learners. Among the important advantages for adults are the opportunities to enhance their cultural awareness and aesthetic appreciation, improve their employment-related and career advancement situations, increase their capability to contribute as productive members of our workforce, and develop their human potential to lead meaningful personal, family, and social lives.

Mentoring and the Educational System

Mentoring has considerable importance as a means of strengthening the general system of secondary education. Given the difficult issues confronted by our often overburdened educators in the public school system, the mentor-mentee approach offers important assistance in the critical effort to increase student retention and promote educational achievement. Mentors are a source of parallel academic learning because they help support, sustain, and expand the instructional activities conducted within the classroom (Orr, 1987).

As significant role models, mentors also psychologically and emotionally supplement the group experience of large classes and counter the prevalent attitude that "nobody cares," often expressed in words and actions by many frustrated, confused, and directionless individuals in our secondary schools. Students with personal motivation difficulties, academic skills deficiencies, or age-inappropriate behavioral problems can benefit from a close connection with mature adults. In addition, students who are demonstrating commitment to their education can engage in mentoring as a means to enrich and advance their current learning pursuits.

In postsecondary education, mentoring is used as a direct intervention to support the continuing development of adult learners. Especially for those students from disadvantaged or nontraditional backgrounds, the mentoring relationship offers a significant survival bridge into and through what is to them the often very different world of academia. Faculty and staff mentors with "school-smart" knowledge and strategies serve as valuable resources for adult learners with few or no peer reference points to help them maneuver through and succeed in the college environment.

By initially supporting students' continuing enrollment, mentors provide critical assistance to students who might vanish, unnoticed except as dropout statistics. Mentors can then attempt to promote the maximum development of adult learners by helping them to actively participate in fulfilling their personal, academic, and employment goals.

Mentoring and Community-Based Associations

By offering the benefits of their knowledge, experience, concern, and wisdom, mentors provide a valuable service to the general society. A great variety of associations support vital programs that use mentoring principles. These associations range from older national endeavors, such as Big Brothers and Big Sisters, the Boy Scouts and Girl Scouts of America, the National 4-H Council, Outward Bound, Aspira, and the National Association of Police Athletic Leagues, to important newer efforts, such as Philadelphia Futures' Sponsor-A-Scholar program and the Ford Foundation's Quantum Opportunities program. Although the terminology used to describe the participants in these programs may be different from "mentors" and "mentees," by enabling direct interaction to occur, these programs all support the development of relationships in which concerned citizens can be active role models to youngsters (Schlossberg, Lynch, and Chickering, 1989).

Mentoring and Internship Training Programs

The official tradition of interns, of mandated continuing students under the close supervision of instructors, is well established in many professional fields, such as education, science, medicine, and mental health. A professional functioning as a teacher usually provides direct instruction and bases critiques of the learner's performance and progress on accepted and standardized criteria. Internship approaches to education clearly provide vital personal exposure to the applied technical aspects of a discipline.

As a role model who represents the profession, the internship instructor significantly affects the overall value of the learning experience. Because the valuable expertise of the instructor is communicated to the learner through ongoing dialogues and specific hands-on demonstrations, the instructor's interpersonal behaviors can dramatically influence the learner as a new practitioner. Instructors not only demonstrate the mastery of expected technical knowledge and proficiency but also reveal the proper attitudes and behaviors associated with performance of professional responsibilities. Thus, for the learner, a cluster of highly relevant educational messages is embedded in the internship experience.

Internship instructors who function as mentors, therefore, provide enriched learning opportunities and enable their adult learners to benefit from all the potential offered by the internship model. The concept of the complete mentor role is compatible with instructor-intern professional training and can enhance the total value of the critically important learning provided by an internship.

Mentoring in the Workplace

The factory model of a strict superior-subordinate hierarchy is a relic of a vanishing industrial world. In business and government, deliberate downsizing and restructuring have resulted in the emergence of fewer managers and smaller staffs, and not surprisingly, the most desirable employees are viewed as self-delegating workers with multifunctional expertise (Baskett and Marsick, 1992).

As one positive outcome of this change, members of management are now expected to function more as collaborative and interactive professionals than ever before (Sayles, 1993). Employees or staff who were once viewed primarily as subordinates are openly defined as competent professionals capable of initiating and completing complex tasks. Even those with authority who previously enjoyed acting as petty tyrants grunting commands must deal with this new and more productive reality. Aware and sensible middle managers and frontline supervisors who were once discouraged from pursuing the mentoring approach in the workplace can now properly assume more of the work-related educational responsibilities associated with the mentor role, such as making available continuing on-the-job training.

Mentoring offers a number of important opportunities to utilize the talent available within these redesigned organizations more intelligently. Although some traditional managerial functions remain necessary, the manager as mentor presents a very positive alternative to authoritarian roles. The daily work of managers can be expanded into productive avenues by orienting managers toward the significant contribution offered by the synergistic process: managers can generate the organizing energy that ignites and combines the work of single individuals and small teams in order to produce the larger overall service or product that the organization offers to its customers.

Managers who increasingly shift into the dual role of manager and educator, working with people who are both employees and adult learners, can function as more constructive orchestrators of human resources than they did before (Sayles, 1993). Mentors in these redefined workplace relationships can provide a valuable service to their total organization by increasing staff members' effectiveness and efficiency and their ability to function as skilled, independent, and collaborative workers.

By creating a positive organizational climate, mentors also stabilize morale and center the productive focus of employees. Staff who define themselves as competent problem solvers are better able to cope with abrupt and stressful transitions because they can channel the high anxiety levels created by uncertainty about the future into the positive energy needed to maintain current creativity and determination (Marsick, 1987). Rather than allow negative psychological and emotional undercurrents to remain unacknowledged and thus to de-energize the workforce by draining employees' capabilities, mentors seek to consciously assist employees to operate productively within changing work and marketplace realities.

Mentoring and On-the-Job Training

Mentoring also applies to the category of education in the workplace usually referred to as *on-the-job training*. Managers are frequently hard-pressed to find instructional time themselves or are reluctant to assign their high achievers another task—that of teaching a new or transferred employee. Scarcity of the resources of time and expertise turns many on-the-job training programs into little more than superficial and nonproductive rituals. And the pressure of operational deadlines and volume of work sometimes even degrades the essential trial, error, and self-correction process of normal instruction into a punitive experience for the learner.

Today's complex competitive reality requires that astute organizations maximize rather than minimize a major internal training resource—the capacity of their own staff to intelligently function at all levels as on-the-job mentors. To survive, organizations must maintain a knowledge of continually upgraded and sophisticated technology, stay current on the high-speed global information superhighway, and anticipate and respond to the rapidly changing requirements of demanding customers.

Exposure to the principles of sound mentoring practice benefits both managers and nonmanagers. As an essential component of staff development, on-the-job learning enables individuals to adapt quickly to change and to sustain the ongoing variety of competencies that are essential survival qualities. By offering pragmatic guidelines that directly apply to on-the-job training, the one-to-one adult learning model improves the ability of organizations to utilize their already available in-house talent. When mentoring interaction is a fully integrated component of life in the workplace, it genuinely contributes to productivity and enables organizations to compete more successfully for customers.

Mentors as Learners in the Workplace

Mentoring provides an opportunity for managers to learn directly from the staff. Many employees still take a rather cynical view of the sincerity of managers who say they really consider employee input. Mentor-mentee interaction provides a forum in which individuals can actively improve their interpersonal skills by realistically practicing the art of understanding others. By promoting the trust required for staff to contribute their genuinely productive ideas and substantive personal concerns, mentoring dialogues reduce negative speculation about hidden motives and accelerate meaningful workplace interpersonal learning. Mentor-mentee relationships encourage employees to appreciate that their views are welcomed and important. The receptive climate generally created by the mentoring relationship stimulates staff to offer valuable suggestions that they may no longer be prepared to offer under the old static suggestion box concept or even as part of the newer incentive package approach to rewarding workable suggestions.

When there has been a continuing dialogue based on respectful and genuine commitment to explore and understand different points of view, both managers and nonmanagers are more likely to recognize the legitimate difficulties inherent in resolving problems and arriving at solutions that satisfy mutual interests. Although the mentoring model of one-to-one relationships does not guarantee agreement about all problems or issues, it does encourage a rational means of reducing misinterpretation due to unfounded assumptions or naïve expectations. Individuals learn together how to discuss positively those suggestions that are not viewed by all as feasible, workable, or even desirable, as well as to deal with the fact that every individual request will not be followed by an affirmative response.

The mentor-mentee concept applies to the workplace because all staff members must function as continuing adult learners if they are to perform at their maximum and allow their organization to successfully compete in a highly demanding marketplace. Employees collectively determine if tough, results-oriented internal and external customers are satisfied. Today, such customers, under pressure themselves to supply services and products, have neither the time nor the resources to cope with excuses. It should come as no surprise when people in our society become openly hostile to incompetent providers and immediately seek other sources. Customers under stress will simply not tolerate paying people to create more stress for them.

Mentoring can be a means of establishing vital work-related relationships that promote acquired learning between employees, whether or not these relationships are officially labeled as on-the-job training programs. If properly utilized, the mentoring model of learning can help employees maintain the essential current knowledge, skills, and professional behaviors required of the modern competitive or public service enterprise. Workplace relationships enhanced by mentoring can also assist in the continuing development of human resources within the organization and increase the organization's overall pragmatic strength to provide marketable future services and products.

Employees viewed as reasonable and maturing individuals who are capable of benefiting from multiple approaches to education are well served by the mentoring experience. However, staff development programs based on a narrow perception of employees as only valuable commodities to be trained (or acted upon) actually distort the essential needs of adults as interactive learners.

The tunnel vision view of employees as on the receiving end only of on-the-job training usually results in less than meaningful or coherent learning because it severely limits the essential active participation required for teaching and learning complex skills and for promoting independent decision making.

Mentoring assists in personalizing and enriching human resource development relationships at work and contributes to the creation of more respectful, collaborative, productive, and satisfying staff interactions. The legitimate economic interests of the organization—to create profit and thereby to sustain itself—can be seen as compatible with the legitimate self-interest of employees in their own personal and career goals. Such a self-reinforcing, positive workplace climate is an especially desirable reality in increasingly stressful and competitive times.

Mentoring and Issues of Equity

A number of barriers, such as gender and ethnicity, have often prevented the spontaneous pairing of mentors and mentees in our learning society. Gender has been a historical obstacle in this culture because males were dominant in most positions of significant authority. The classic definition of the mentor as a wiser, experienced, and expert traveler on the road the mentee also wished to travel therefore placed males rather than females in the visible situation of career advocate (Jeruchim and Shapiro, 1992).

Moreover, even males with proper motives prefer not to approach younger females with the offer to serve as mentors in one-to-one relationships because of the sexual innuendoes often attributed to their initiatives. Conversely, females are reluctant to approach older males to seek genuine assistance because such requests can be misinterpreted by males or viewed with suspicion by co-workers. Even a strictly conducted professional mentoring relationship can still create impressions of impropriety, generate gossip, and even stigmatize the participants when it develops between males and females. Given this reality, males have generally mentored other males, and females have been faced with seeking mentors from among a much smaller pool of visible female executives. This imbalance has frequently caused females to be disenfranchised as candidates for mentoring.

However, when a mentoring program is sponsored by an organization and the mentors therefore represent the organization, an official environment is established in which mentoring can flourish. Administrators assume responsibility for planning, organizing, and implementing interactions with clearly defined objectives and guidelines, and they can ensure that direct channels for negative feedback are available to all participants. If difficulties arise, this approach allows for immediate and effective intervention into incipient problems without precipitating mentor-mentee overreactions.

The sponsored program promotes relevant mentor-mentee involvement that probably would never occur if it were not in the context of a sanctioned relationship. With proper safeguards, relevant orientations, and substantive mentor training, the mentoring relationship contributes to the maturation of mentees as adult learners. Mentoring nurtured in an enlightened environment can be meaningfully extended to the pursuit of continuing learning in society at large.

Other important influences on the mentoring relationship, such as ethnicity, age, and socioeconomic background can be approached from several perspectives. First, differences that foster stereotyping by either of the participants obviously require examination because they prevent the development of meaningful mentor-mentee relationships and thereby detract from the attainment of mentee goals. The mentoring dialogue, when used with knowledge and sensitivity by mentors, offers the power of direct exposure to the differences represented by others. The recognition that people contain a multitude of legitimate, positive, and exciting differences is an intrinsically valuable part of the learning experience.

Second, the mentoring relationship offers an opportunity for both mentors and mentees to learn how to explore real-world differences between them, differences that often are not obvious. When participants have similar backgrounds, they usually are more immediately comfortable with each other. But mentors and mentees must maintain sensitivity over the long haul of the developing relationship. When paired individuals are initially comfortable with each other primarily because of their similarities, then both must learn not to be lulled by their visible sameness into naïve assumptions about the ease with which the goals of mentoring will be realized. They must be realistically prepared for the understandable discomfort that will be created by their increasingly noticeable differences as their mentoring relationship evolves.

Mentoring and the Learning Society

The learning relationship that is mentoring is centered in respectful one-to-one interaction. And the broad vision of that learning relationship is generalizable to our larger society. It shows how learners can be presented with positive direction, support, and challenge as they journey through the worlds of business, government, and education. Mentoring relationships wherever they occur promote meaningful understanding and appreciation of multicultural and other differences; they also allow mentors to demonstrate the behavior involved in resolving issues between persons who appear similar to each other but are dissimilar in not so obvious ways.

Mentoring is a philosophical vision as well as a pragmatic approach to guiding adults through one-to-one learning. The challenge for mentors is to effectively share their expertise and significantly enhance the growth of mentees from all backgrounds. Mentors offer valuable contributions to the personal, educational, and career development of mentees as individual citizens and to the collective enrichment of our culture.

References

Baskett, H.K.M., and Marsick, V. J. (eds.). *Professionals' Ways of Knowing: New Findings on How to Improve Professional Education.* New Directions for Adult and Continuing Education, no. 55. San Francisco: Jossey-Bass, 1992.

Brookfield, S. D. "Grounding Teaching in Learning." In M. W. Galbraith (ed.), *Facilitating Adult Learning: A Transactional Process*. Malabar, Fla.: Krieger, 1991.

Cohen, N. H. *Mentoring Adult Learners: A Guide for Educators and Trainers*. Malabar, Fla.: Krieger, 1995.

Daloz, L. A. *Effective Teaching and Mentoring: Realizing the Transformational Power of Adult Learning Experiences*. San Francisco: Jossey-Bass, 1986.

Galbraith, M. W. "The Adult Learning Transactional Process." In M. W. Galbraith (ed.), *Facilitating Adult Learning: A Transactional Process*. Malabar, Fla.: Krieger, 1991.

Jeruchim, J., and Shapiro, P. *Women, Mentors, and Success*. New York: Fawcett/Columbine, 1992.

Marsick, V. J. (ed.). *Learning in the Workplace*. New York: Croom Helm, 1987.

Orr, M. T. *Keeping Students in School: A Guide to Effective Dropout Prevention Programs and Services*. San Francisco: Jossey-Bass, 1987.

Sayles, L. R. *The Working Leader.* New York: Macmillan, 1993.

Schlossberg, N. K., Lynch, A. Q., and Chickering, A. W. *Improving Higher Education Environments for Adults: Responsive Programs and Services from Entry to Departure*. San Francisco: Jossey-Bass, 1989.

NORMAN H. COHEN is associate professor of English at the Community College of Philadelphia.

MICHAEL W. GALBRAITH is professor of adult education in the Department of Educational Leadership at Florida Atlantic University in Boca Raton.

A scale for self-assessment of mentor competencies, an explanation of specific behaviors required for effective mentoring practice, and guidelines for continuing education programs for mentors are presented.

The Principles of Adult Mentoring Scale

Norman H. Cohen

The critical importance of lifelong learning is a general tenet of adult and continuing education, especially in a rapidly changing culture (Beder, 1989; Brookfield, 1986; Galbraith and Zelenak, 1989; Schön, 1987). Professionals, in particular, are viewed as benefiting from learning activities that not only enable them to assimilate new concepts and pragmatic information but also help them to apply such knowledge directly to the world of their empirical practice.

However, professionals usually need to reconsider their ideas and attitudes about the type of preparation that will actually assist them in performing as effective mentors. Advocates for this reorientation (Baskett, Marsick, and Cervero, 1992, p. 114) suggest that mentors will often be required to modify their traditional approach to training in a way that "calls for a departure from the prevailing assumptions imbedded in CPE (continuing professional education) practice, that is, what the learner does is more important than what the instructor does."

To prepare for the mentor role, professionals must engage in the critical first step—the self-assessment of their individual mentoring competencies. In addition, they must be receptive to genuinely exploring other legitimate sources of training that are proposed as relevant to improving their proficiencies as mentor practitioners. In examining the mentoring model of learning, this chapter will cover the need for mentors to engage in self-assessment of their own proficiencies, the issue of evaluation as a factor in developing a professional identity, the function and goals of the mentor role, a scale designed to be an educational reference point for mentor self-development, the integration of that scale into continuing mentor education programs, and the responsibilities of seminar facilitators in conducting training to promote effective mentoring practice.

Need for Mentor Self-Assessment

For professionals to perform effectively as mentors, they must possess sufficient knowledge of adult psychology as well as reasonable individual expertise in interpersonal communication skills (Daloz, 1986; Hurst and Pratt, 1984). However, in reviewing the issue of mentor training in the literature of adult and higher education and counseling, critics have concluded that very little, if any, significant education has directly prepared the majority of professionals in postsecondary education for the complexity of the mentor role (Schlossberg, Lynch, and Chickering, 1989).

Moreover, new mentors may not always give high priority to the need to pursue information and specific training about the influence of the mentor, even though others, such as program administrators and experienced mentor staff, believe that participation in relevant continuing education clearly improves the competencies of mentor practitioners. Many professionals may therefore enter into the mentor role with their concerns about improving the quality of the mentoring experience essentially tilted in the direction of observing and commenting on what students do.

Generally, professional faculty development pursuits are considered similar to interactions between peers, and new mentors may understandably anticipate that mentor training, in contrast, will be much more centered on exploring the activities of mentees and much less preoccupied with examining and critiquing the behaviors of mentors. But the transactional dynamics of one-to-one mentoring assume a relationship based on active rather than passive mentor input.

Both those presenting and those attending training seminars must recognize the problem that will be created if there is too much focus on analyzing the performance of the person in the student role (mentee) and too little focus on understanding the importance of the individual in the teacher role (mentor). If the mentoring experience is to truly benefit the mentee, training programs must avoid an imbalance of emphasis on the significant contribution of the mentor, an imbalance that could seriously limit the enriched learning opportunities that derive as much from mentor initiatives as from mentee responses and actions.

As adult learners, credentialed educators involved in continuing learning about mentoring would be best served if they were exposed to a balanced training experience. Such an approach should include the recognition that responsibility for meaningful mentoring cannot reasonably be reduced to a formula based only on scrutinizing the side of the equation labeled "mentee actions."

Professional Identity

Another concern raised by the issue of professional self-assessment and development is that most faculty derive their sense of themselves as important in the lives of their students from the classroom experience. This context can present a potential problem because the professionals involved may have an unclear, inaccurate, or distorted sense of their own effectiveness as positive influences in their work with groups of students.

As solo practitioners operating almost exclusively in the world of classroom interactions, postsecondary faculty are particularly characterized by some critics as insufficiently prepared to conduct or participate in meaningful self-evaluation or self-development to improve their skills as instructors (Civikly, 1986). Such a sweeping criticism invites the risk of being dismissed as too harshly judgmental. Nevertheless, if for many faculty recruited as mentors the classroom is an uncritical and unexamined domain of assumed professional competence and if that classroom is their reference point, then what kind of transition are they likely to make into the intensely personal world of one-to-one interaction as a faculty mentor to adult learners?

Mentor practitioners must recognize that the mentoring model of learning extends beyond the basic assumption that student behavior is of more central concern than teacher behavior. To assume the professional identity of a mentor is to fully comprehend and apply the equally important idea that what mentors do also considerably influences the learning of mentees. Perhaps this point should be apparent to all, but as an eminent thinker, Oliver Wendell Holmes, Jr. (1980, p. 644) observed back in 1913, we often "need education in the obvious."

In fact, an acknowledged pioneer in the field of adult education (Knowles, 1970, p. 41) stressed over twenty years ago that the "behavior of the teacher probably influences the character of the learning climate more than any other single factor." And more recently, an often-referenced authority (Daloz, 1986, p. 244) asserted that "far more than any other factor, it is the partnership of teacher and student that finally determines the value of an education. In the nurture of that partnership lies the mentor's art." As participant role models, mentors must acknowledge their own considerable power to create a relatively positive or negative experience—certainly from the learner's point of view—within the collaborative sphere of the mentoring relationship.

Mentor Role

The mentor role in postsecondary education is based on a synthesis of those mentoring behaviors in the adult and higher education literature that are considered essential for the development of meaningful mentor-mentee relationships (Cohen, 1993). The idea of learning as a transaction—an interactive and evolving process between mentors and their adult learners—is considered a fundamental component of the adult mentoring relationship (Brookfield, 1986; Daloz, 1986; Galbraith, 1991). Effective mentors are viewed as possessing interpersonal competency. And this perception of the mentor as a professional who is a skilled one-to-one behavioral practitioner parallels the portrait of the instructor as a professional who demonstrates proficient teaching and group-process skills in the classroom.

A major assumption of mentoring, of the one-to-one model of interaction, is that its purpose is to develop mentor-mentee learning guided by educational rather than therapeutic principles and goals (Cohen, 1993, 1995). Another important premise is that the adult mentoring experience is based on a model of learning that understands that it is the behavioral role of the mentor that in fact makes a mentor-mentee interaction an adult mentoring relationship. However, the mentoring model of learning also sees mentees as responsible for assuming a significant degree of personal involvement as participant adult learners in their own developmental journeys. A clear emphasis, therefore, on mentor behavior is not intended to minimize the accountability of the mentee as a learner but rather to maximize the contribution of the mentor as a vital participant in the learning process—to highlight what the mentor does as an influence (Cohen, 1995).

Purpose of the Principles of Adult Mentoring Scale

The Principles of Adult Mentoring Scale (Appendix A) is based on a composite profile of the complete mentor role. It is a self-assessment instrument designed primarily for use by professionals who have consciously assumed mentoring responsibilities in their relationships with adult learners. (This chapter presents the postsecondary version of the Principles of Adult Mentoring Scale; a government and business version can be found in Cohen, 1995.)

The scale assesses the mentor functions and behaviors that experts in postsecondary education agree are most likely to be of significance in relationships between mentors such as faculty, counselors, and administrators and their adult mentee learners. It evaluates fifty-five specific mentor interpersonal behaviors relevant to establishing and maintaining an evolving mentoring relationship. It also provides both scholars and mentor practitioners with a baseline from which they can document, analyze, understand, and improve professional mentoring practice.

Scoring the Scale. After all fifty-five statements included in the Principles of Adult Mentoring Scale have been answered based on the five possible choices, three separate activities are required to complete the process of scoring. First, instructions for scoring (Appendix B) are used to guide the development of scale scores. Second, the scores are entered on a scoring sheet (Appendix C) that converts the answers into clusters of numerical information and places them under six separate mentor functions. Finally, the results of the scoring sheet are recorded on a mentor role competency form (Appendix D) to reveal the overall scale score, as well as the separate scores for each of the six mentor function categories.

Interpreting the Scale. Finally, the taxonomy of the mentor role (Appendix E) is used as the reference point for understanding mentoring behaviors. It contains the following information: six categories of separate but interrelated mentor functions considered as critical to success in the mentoring relationship; definition and purpose statements that explain the rationale for and observable actions of each distinct function; and lists of the actual verbal and nonverbal communication behaviors typical of each function that a mentor would demonstrate with an adult learner.

When professionals consider the implications of their mentoring competency ratings (Appendix D), certain basic points should be stressed. Scores in the ranges labeled "not effective" and "less effective" not only indicate an obvious need for improvement but also suggest that there are serious negative mentor behaviors that may create major interpersonal communication barriers if not corrected. For instance, mentors should be particularly alert to low scores in relationship behaviors and attitudes and high scores in confrontive ones, a combination that may reveal too little attention to critical relationship functions and too much investment in confrontive focus behaviors.

While an extreme mentoring scenario by no means automatically follows from such scores, such imbalances explain how the potential of mentoring to generate productive learning could be undermined. Such an out-of-balance mentor profile, in which confrontation occurs in a chilly relational atmosphere, could produce a counterproductive impact, inhibiting a mentee's ability to appropriately disclose needs, goals, and problems and therefore to genuinely trust those who officially represent institutions.

A score in the "effective" category reveals a general competency in the function being reviewed. From the mentee's perspective, the effective mentor would usually be experienced as demonstrating concern and offering assistance through appropriate observable behavior. However, as an illustration of a less-than-obvious implication, an acceptable confrontive score may sometimes (depending on the overall mentor profile) suggest that a mentor has a tendency to remain within the comfort zone of adequate confrontational behavior and to avoid the discomfort often associated with the upper ranges of appropriately confrontive mentor-mentee interaction. For instance, a mentor very high in the relationship and information ranges but average in confrontive behavior could be very effective in the nurturing dimension but less successful when the confrontive component—the proper pointing out of discrepancies—was necessary.

Scores in the "very effective" and "highly effective" areas, of course, indicate rather sophisticated mentoring behavioral skills, which could still be fine tuned since the effective side of the continuum does not imply perfection. Mentors whose overall profiles show highly effective mentoring skills might consider volunteering early in collaborative training seminars to role-play helpful mentoring behaviors and to participate in constructive critiques of participants' particular ideas, attitudes, and techniques.

Development of the Scale

The Principles of Adult Mentoring Scale was formulated to provide mentors with a valid and reliable instrument for use in examining their own mentoring competencies. A comprehensive review of significant scholarly publications clearly indicated the need for a self-assessment scale that could promote the continuing professional education of staff who had assumed responsibility for the mentoring of adult mentees in postsecondary education (Cohen, 1993).

The definition of the contemporary mentor role and the descriptions of the six behavioral functions were derived from an analysis of the relevant adult education (and related) literature. Authoritative references and experts in the fields of research design, scale construction, and statistical evaluation were used to guide each stage of scale development. Reliability analysis, which tests for the internal consistency of item statements (computed on a scale between 0 and 1), revealed an alpha of .9490 for the Principles of Adult Mentoring Scale (Cohen, 1993).

Use of the Scale for Continuing Learning

Continuing education seminars could emphasize mutual learning between professionals and thereby offer opportunities for expanding the personal self-assessment information provided by the scale (Cohen, 1995). For example, participants could create a directly shared mentoring experience by engaging in role simulations and then basing their evaluative comments on the behavioral guidelines proposed in Appendix E. Also, the content of the fifty-five scale statements (Appendix A) could be used as the basis for examining topics representative of mentor-mentee dialogue.

The scale and its associated materials could be used in seminars to focus participants on a highly specific mentor behavioral competency, review one or more distinct mentor functions, and evaluate an individual's overall performance in the complete mentor role (all six functions). Initially, the purpose and scope of the mentor role could serve as the center of discussion on understanding the essentials of mentoring practice. But the seminars should also explore other topics such as the influence of authority, gender, ethnicity, age, and socioeconomic background on the mentoring relationship (Cohen, 1995).

Responsibility of Seminar Facilitator

In learning to function in the mentor role, professionals should remain ready to question the purpose and value of the content and methods that are employed at mentor training seminars. They may even need to respectfully challenge the knowledge and experience of those offering the training in which they are asked to participate, especially as it applies to the highly significant behavioral dimension of mentoring.

Certainly, the theory and practice of mentoring will be a central point of discussion at the continuing education seminars for new mentors. The ability of those conducting the seminars to create a positive educational and psychological environment will have a significant impact on the perceived value of the training program as a meaningful participatory learning experience. Those selected to represent the organization as "trainers" and facilitators must therefore be viewed as important influences on the professionals who are learning how to become effective mentors.

The ability of the seminar facilitator to establish the necessary positive climate should therefore be given serious consideration, because the early attitudes formed by mentors toward continuing training will impact on such realities as their subsequent attendance and involvement. Also, the facilitator's substantive knowledge about mentoring, expertise in one-to-one interpersonal skills, and experience in conducting small-group training sessions will certainly be a major factor in contributing to improved mentoring effectiveness.

For example, in an interactive seminar, the facilitator and other experienced mentors could review the six mentor functions in Appendix E and demonstrate various mentor-mentee behaviors for critique before the whole group. Then, new mentors could participate in role-plays with the more knowledgeable mentors. And finally, all the mentors, in groups of three or four, could rotate in the roles of both mentor and mentee. After every individual had participated in a simulated mentoring situation, each small group could exchange internal feedback, and then the seminar facilitator could assist the entire group in exploring their collective experience with mentoring behavior.

It is vital, of course, that the person being evaluated remain open to the critiques and neither resort to overly defensive verbal responses nor withdraw into resentful silence. In conducting the training sessions, the facilitator could use the technique of consensual validation as a means of balancing and integrating the differing and even opposing views of the participants. This approach promotes positive group interactions and constructive exchanges of viewpoints and thus encourages the individual being critiqued to benefit from multiple feedback.

To use this technique, the facilitator initially points out, without overstating the point or attempting to improperly control the interaction, that although any mentor may certainly refer to another person's critique as merely that of a single and subjective perception, each mentor should also be prepared to consider the collaborative responses of peers as containing a reasonable percentage of objective, factually grounded, and reality-based significance. An important goal of consensual validation is to minimize the tendency of participants to shut down emotionally by giving them guidelines for monitoring inappropriately critical communication by specific individuals within the group, thus ensuring that the potential for relevant mutual learning is maximized for all.

In offering comments, the participants must be careful to respect different points of view. A critique should be regarded as an interpretation of another mentor's unique style of mentoring, not as an opportunity to win an argument. In learning the mentor's art, the primary issue to initially explore is the extent to which a mentor fulfills the baseline requirements of effective mentoring practice. The facilitator can also use the baseline requirements to resolve problems of inaccurate self-assessment, especially with mentors who have a tendency to under- or overestimate their own proficiencies in mentoring relationships.

Also, in the attempt to engage the group in constructive dialogue, the facilitator must ensure that the integrity of the mentor being evaluated not be raised as an issue. In offering a critique, an observer's central concern should be the probable impact of the mentor's observable behaviors on the mentee. Mentors are assumed to operate out of proper motives, and speculative comments about the sincerity or honesty of a mentor's personal intentions are relevant only if such feedback is connected to the possibility of mentee misinterpretation or distortion of a mentor's good intentions due to ineffective mentoring behaviors. If evidence of actual improper behavior should surface, then the facilitator and program administrators would, of course, pursue the matter.

Finally, the videotaping of participants is another option that can enhance the value of mentor training. Obviously, this approach requires a clear sensitivity to the readiness of each particular individual to benefit from the experience. Assuming a continuing education model based on a series of scheduled seminars, video would be introduced into the training program only after the mentors had the opportunity to exchange their views and were reasonably comfortable with each other. Again, the six factors in Appendix E could guide a critique of individual mentor performance.

In general, mentors will benefit most from factual and tolerant feedback that offers them an opportunity to reflect on and respond to the specific observations of their peers. Use of the six factors will help ensure that seminar participants all use the same criteria for evaluating mentoring behaviors. Critiques that are genuinely and sufficiently balanced and comprehensive will promote constructive dialogue and enrich the shared learning experience among professionals.

Conclusion

Mentoring is viewed as highly relevant to promoting the continuing development of adults in our learning society, and its principles are generalizable to academic, business, government, and community settings. Professionals functioning in the complete mentor role offer the active participation necessary for the creation of meaningful mentoring relationships that enrich and advance adult learning. Mentees benefit from direct one-to-one interaction with concerned professionals who are committed to help them pursue personal, educational, and career objectives. Mentoring, as a holistic learning experience, enables mentees to learn and apply the adaptive skills necessary for handling the complexity of change in our culture.

The Principles of Adult Mentoring Scale is designed to help professionals assess their own competencies in the mentor role. Scale results offer a guide to the continuing education options professionals might individually choose to enhance their own proficiencies in the mentor's art. Moreover, as an attempt to establish and clarify effective mentor behaviors, the scale, along with its associated information, is valuable as an educational source that helps professionals understand the behaviors of effective mentoring practice. With proper attention directed toward meeting the adult learning needs of the professionals who participate, the scale materials can also be used as a component of more formal training programs for mentors.

Appendix A:
Principles of Adult Mentoring Scale:
Postsecondary Education

Instructions for Completion

A. Circle *one* of the following choices for each of the following 55 statements. Choose the one that is *most representative of your actual behavior as a mentor.**

Never   Infrequently   Sometimes   Frequently   Always

*Note: If you have functioned as a mentor, your answers should be based on your past (and, if applicable, current) mentoring experience. If you have very little or no actual experience as a mentor of adults, your answers should be based on how you would probably interact at this time with a mentee.

B. Answer all of the statements, then refer to the instructions for scoring and interpreting located at the end of the scale [Appendixes B through E].

Scale Statements

1. I encourage students to express their honest feelings (positive and negative) about their academic and social experiences as adult learners in college.

Never   Infrequently   Sometimes   Frequently   Always

2. I discuss with students who are discouraged (due to poor scholastic performance or other difficulties) the importance of developing a realistic view of learning that can include both success and disappointment (mentioning other students who have been frustrated as learners but have continued their education).

Never   Infrequently   Sometimes   Frequently   Always

3. I ask students for detailed information about their academic progress.

Never   Infrequently   Sometimes   Frequently   Always

4. I refer students to other staff members and departments to obtain information they need about academic and career plans.

Never   Infrequently   Sometimes   Frequently   Always

5. I attempt to be verbally supportive when students are emotionally upset.

Never   Infrequently   Sometimes   Frequently   Always

6. I suggest to students that we establish a regular schedule of meeting times.

Never   Infrequently   Sometimes   Frequently   Always

7. I make a good deal of eye contact with students.

Never   Infrequently   Sometimes   Frequently   Always

8. I suggest that students who indicate concerns about serious emotional or psychological problems meet with a college counselor.

Never   Infrequently   Sometimes   Frequently   Always

9. I ask students to explain (in some detail) the reasons for their college plans and career choices.

Never   Infrequently   Sometimes   Frequently   Always

10. I encourage students to provide a good deal of background information about their academic preparation, success, and problems in college.

Never   Infrequently   Sometimes   Frequently   Always

11. I inquire in some depth about students' study strategies and (if necessary) offer practical suggestions and/or refer them for help to improve their academic performance.

Never   Infrequently   Sometimes   Frequently   Always

12. I explain to students that I really want to know what they as individuals honestly think about issues (such as balancing college commitments and outside responsibilities) so that I can offer advice specific to them.

Never   Infrequently   Sometimes   Frequently   Always

13. I arrange my meetings (when possible) with students at times when I will probably not be interrupted very much by telephone calls or other people.

Never   Infrequently   Sometimes   Frequently   Always

14. I explain the need to explore degree and career options to students who have insufficient information (such as adult learners in transition between job fields or facing long-term commitments to fulfill degree requirements).

Never   Infrequently   Sometimes   Frequently   Always

15. I encourage students to consider nontraditional (such as television-based) courses as well as more formal educational opportunities they have not yet explored to develop their personal interests.

Never   Infrequently   Sometimes   Frequently   Always

16. I point out inconsistencies (rationalizations) in students' explanations of why their academic goals were not achieved if I believe my comments will help them develop better coping strategies to deal with their problem.

Never   Infrequently   Sometimes   Frequently   Always

17. I try to stimulate students to do more rigorous critical thinking about the long-range implications (time commitments, life-style changes) their academic choices may have for increasing the complexity of their lives.

Never   Infrequently   Sometimes   Frequently   Always

18. I explain to students why they should discuss (even with someone else) significant academic problems they are presently confronted with even if they prefer not to deal with these issues.

Never   Infrequently   Sometimes   Frequently   Always

19. I offer recommendations to students about their personal academic learning needs (from remedial to honors courses, tutoring, course loads) based on specific information provided by them (as well as placement tests and academic records, if available) during our meetings.

Never   Infrequently   Sometimes   Frequently   Always

20. I follow up on students' decisions to develop better personal strategies (study habits, getting accurate information, making realistic decisions) by asking questions (and offering comments, if appropriate) about their actual progress at later meetings.

Never   Infrequently   Sometimes   Frequently   Always

21. I tell students when I think their ideas about career or academic concerns (such as job entry or degree requirements) are very clearly based on incomplete or inaccurate information.

Never   Infrequently   Sometimes   Frequently   Always

22. I attempt to guide students in exploring their own personal commitment to career or academic interests by posing alternative views for them to consider.

Never   Infrequently   Sometimes   Frequently   Always

23. I verbally communicate my concerns to students when their negative attitudes and emotions are expressed to me through such nonverbal behaviors as eye contact, facial expression, and voice tone.

Never   Infrequently   Sometimes   Frequently   Always

24. I discuss students' general reasons for attending college and then focus on helping them identify concrete educational objectives, degrees, curricula, and courses.

Never   Infrequently   Sometimes   Frequently   Always

25. I provide a reasonable amount of guidance in our discussions so that students will explore realistic options and attainable academic and career objectives.

Never   Infrequently   Sometimes   Frequently   Always

26. I ask students to review their strategies for managing the changes in their lives (such as impact of increased time pressures on personal relationships or ability to handle current jobs) while they pursue their "dreams" regarding educational goals.

Never   Infrequently   Sometimes   Frequently   Always

27. I question students' assumptions (especially about career options and the value of education) as a way of guiding them through a realistic appraisal of the extent to which their important ideas and beliefs are based on adequate personal experiences and facts.

Never   Infrequently   Sometimes   Frequently   Always

28. I discuss my own work-related experience as a way of helping students think about and carefully examine their career options.

Never   Infrequently   Sometimes   Frequently   Always

29. I share with students personal examples of difficulties I have overcome in my own individual and professional growth if these experiences might provide insights for them.

Never   Infrequently   Sometimes   Frequently   Always

30. I engage students in discussions that require them to reflect on the new competencies they will need to achieve their future goals.

Never   Infrequently   Sometimes   Frequently   Always

31. I point out (using personal examples as well as stories about students) that achievement in college is primarily based on personal commitment (rather than just "luck"), to students who are having problems completing the work but appear unrealistic about the amount of discipline and energy needed to cope with the pressures of an academic workload.

Never   Infrequently   Sometimes   Frequently   Always

32. I express my personal confidence in the ability of students to succeed if they persevere in the pursuit of their academic goals.

Never   Infrequently   Sometimes   Frequently   Always

33. I confront students with the reality of continued or probable negative consequences in a direct (but supportive) manner when they repeatedly do not follow through on their stated intentions to deal with serious academic problems.

Never   Infrequently   Sometimes   Frequently   Always

34. I encourage students to use me as a sounding board to explore their hopes, ideas, feelings, and plans.

Never   Infrequently   Sometimes   Frequently   Always

35. I engage students in discussions aimed at motivating them to develop a positive view of their ability to function now and in the future as independent, competent adult learners.

Never   Infrequently   Sometimes   Frequently   Always

36. I use my own experience (personal as well as references to other students I have advised) to explain how college courses or activities students believe will be boring, too demanding, or not relevant could be valuable learning experiences for them.

Never   Infrequently   Sometimes   Frequently   Always

37. I offer students constructive criticism if I believe their avoidance of problems and decisions is clearly limiting their growth as adult learners.

Never   Infrequently   Sometimes   Frequently   Always

38. I encourage students to make well-informed personal choices as they plan their own educational and career goals.

Never   Infrequently   Sometimes   Frequently   Always

39. I explore with students who express a lack of confidence in themselves the ways in which their own life experience might be a valuable resource to help them devise strategies to succeed within the college environment.

Never   Infrequently   Sometimes   Frequently   Always

40. I assist students in using facts to carefully map out realistic step-by-step strategies to achieve their academic and career goals.

Never   Infrequently   Sometimes   Frequently   Always

41. I share my own views and feelings when they are relevant to the college-related situations and issues I am discussing with students.

Never   Infrequently   Sometimes   Frequently   Always

42. I listen to criticism from students about college policies, regulations, requirements, and even colleagues without immediately attempting to offer justifications.

Never   Infrequently   Sometimes   Frequently   Always

43. I offer comments to students about their inappropriate behavior (in college) if I have a reasonable expectation that they are prepared to work on positive change and will most likely experience some success as a result.

Never   Infrequently   Sometimes   Frequently   Always

44. I inform students that they can discuss "negative" emotions such as anxiety, self-doubt, fear, and anger in our meetings.

Never   Infrequently   Sometimes   Frequently   Always

45. I express confidence in students' abilities to achieve their educational goals, especially when they are having personal difficulties in fulfilling their academic responsibilities due to outside pressures (work, family, relationships).

Never   Infrequently   Sometimes   Frequently   Always

46. I question students' decisions and actions regarding college-related issues and problems when they do not appear to be appropriate solutions.

Never   Infrequently   Sometimes   Frequently   Always

47. I discuss the positive and negative feelings students have about their abilities to succeed as adult learners.

Never   Infrequently   Sometimes   Frequently   Always

48. I offer as few carefully chosen criticisms as possible when I try to get students to understand the (often difficult to accept) connection between their own self-limiting (defeating) behaviors and their inability to solve a particular problem.

Never   Infrequently   Sometimes   Frequently   Always

49. I ask probing questions that require more than a yes or no answer, so that students will explain (in some detail) their views regarding their academic progress and plans.

Never   Infrequently   Sometimes   Frequently   Always

50. I explore with students the extent of their commitment (such as willingness to spend time and energy) as adult learners in achieving their educational goals.

Never   Infrequently   Sometimes   Frequently   Always

51. I base the timing of my "confrontive" questions and comments to students on my knowledge of their individual readiness (often related to the stage of our relationship) to benefit from discussions about clearly sensitive issues.

Never   Infrequently   Sometimes   Frequently   Always

52. I discuss my role as a mentor with students so that their individual expectations of me are appropriate and realistic.

Never   Infrequently   Sometimes   Frequently   Always

53. I try to clarify the problems students are explaining to me by verbally expressing my understanding of their feelings and then asking if my views are accurate.

Never   Infrequently   Sometimes   Frequently   Always

54. I ask students to reflect on the resources available (college, family, community) to help them manage their lives effectively while they pursue their educational and career goals.

Never   Infrequently   Sometimes   Frequently   Always

55. I emphasize to students, especially those who appear uncertain about what to expect from our meetings, that one of my important goals is to assist them in reaching their own decisions about personal, academic, and career goals.

Never   Infrequently   Sometimes   Frequently   Always

Appendix B:
Instructions for Scoring

1. Assign point values:

   Never   1 point
   Infrequently   2 points
   Sometimes   3 points
   Frequently   4 points
   Always   5 points

2. Refer to the sheet headed "Scoring Sheet: Postsecondary Education" [Appendix C], which shows the fifty-five items from the scale (identified by number) distributed under the six factors.

3. Under each factor, enter the appropriate point value (1 to 5) on the blank printed below each item number. Then add up the points for each factor and record the cumulative factor score on the "total" blank.

4. Next, total the six separate factor scores and record the cumulative score on the "grand total for overall score" blank.

5. Refer to the sheet headed "Mentor Role Competencies: Postsecondary Education" [Appendix D]. Record the overall composite score and then enter the separate scores (totals) for each of the six factors in the appropriate boxes.

Appendix C:
Scoring Sheet: Postsecondary Education

Factor 1: Relationship Emphasis

Items:	1	5	7	12	13	23	42	44	47	53		Relationship
Points:	—	—	—	—	—	—	—	—	—	—		_____
												(total)

Factor 2: Information Emphasis

Items:	3	4	6	9	10	11	19	24	40	52		Information
Points:	—	—	—	—	—	—	—	—	—	—		_____
												(total)

Factor 3: Facilitative Focus

Items:	15	22	25	34	39	49	Facilitative
Points:	—	—	—	—	—	—	_____
							(total)

Factor 4: Confrontive Focus

Items:	8	16	18	21	27	31	33	37	43	46	48	51	Confrontive
Points:	—	—	—	—	—	—	—	—	—	—	—	—	_____
													(total)

Factor 5: Mentor Model

Items:	2	28	29	32	36	41	Mentor
Points:	—	—	—	—	—	—	_____
							(total)

Factor 6: Student Vision

Items:	14	17	20	26	30	35	38	45	50	54	55	Student
Points:	—	—	—	—	—	—	—	—	—	—	—	_____
												(total)

Grand total overall score: _____

Appendix D:
Mentor Role Competencies: Postsecondary Education

Overall score

55–190	191–205	206–219	220–234	235–275
Not Effective	Less Effective	Effective	Very Effective	Highly Effective

Relationship Emphasis

10–35	36–38	39–41	42–44	45–50
Not Effective	Less Effective	Effective	Very Effective	Highly Effective

Information Emphasis

10–33	34–36	37–39	40–42	43–50
Not Effective	Less Effective	Effective	Very Effective	Highly Effective

Facilitative Focus

6–18	19–20	21–22	23–24	25–30
Not Effective	Less Effective	Effective	Very Effective	Highly Effective

Confrontive Focus

12–39	40–43	44–46	47–50	51–60
Not Effective	Less Effective	Effective	Very Effective	Highly Effective

Mentor Model

6–18	19–21	22–23	24–25	26–30
Not Effective	Less Effective	Effective	Very Effective	Highly Effective

Student Vision

11–37	38–41	42–44	45–47	48–55
Not Effective	Less Effective	Effective	Very Effective	Highly Effective

Appendix E:
The Mentor Role: Six Behavioral Functions

Factor 1: Relationship Emphasis

Conveys through active, empathetic listening a genuine understanding and acceptance of mentees' feelings

Purpose

To create a psychological climate of trust that allows mentees to honestly share and reflect upon their personal experiences (positive and negative) as adult learners

Mentor Behaviors

- Responsive listening (verbal and nonverbal reactions that signal sincere interest)
- Open-ended questions related to expressed immediate concerns about actual situations
- Descriptive feedback based on observations rather than inferences of motive
- Perception checks to ensure comprehension of feelings
- Nonjudgmental sensitive responses to assist in clarification of emotional states and reactions

Factor 2: Information Emphasis

Directly requests detailed information from and offers specific suggestions to mentees about their current plans and progress in achieving personal, educational, and career goals

Purpose

To ensure that advice offered is based on accurate and sufficient knowledge of individual mentees

Mentor Behaviors

- Questions aimed at assuring factual understanding of present educational and career situation
- Review of relevant background to develop adequate personal profile
- Probing questions that require concrete answers

- Directive comments about present problems and solutions that should be considered
- Restatements to ensure factual accuracy and interpretive understanding
- Reliance on facts as an integral component of the decision-making process

Factor 3: Facilitative Focus

Guides mentees through a reasonably in-depth review of and exploration of their interests, abilities, ideas, and beliefs

Purpose

To assist mentees in considering alternative views and options while reaching their own decisions about attainable personal, academic, and career objectives

Mentor Behaviors

- Hypothetical questions to expand individual views
- Uncovering of underlying experiential and information bases for assumptions
- Presentation of multiple viewpoints to generate more in-depth analysis of decisions and options
- Examination of seriousness of commitment to goals
- Analysis of reasons for current pursuits
- Review of recreational and vocational preferences

Factor 4: Confrontive Focus

Respectfully challenges mentees' explanations for or avoidance of decisions and actions relevant to their development as adult learners

Purpose

To help mentees attain insight into unproductive strategies and behaviors and to evaluate their need and capacity to change

Mentor Behaviors

- Careful probing to assess psychological readiness to benefit from different points of view
- Open acknowledgment of concerns about possible negative consequences of constructive ("critical") feedback on relationship
- Confrontive verbal stance aimed at primary goal of promoting self-assessment of apparent discrepancies
- Selective focus on most likely behaviors for meaningful change
- Attention to using least amount of carefully stated feedback necessary for impact
- Comments (offered before and after confrontive remarks) to reinforce belief in positive potential for growth beyond current situation

Factor 5: Mentor Model

Shares (self-discloses) life experiences and feelings as a role model to mentees in order to personalize and enrich the relationship

Purpose

To motivate mentees to take necessary risks (make decisions without certainty of successful results) and to overcome difficulties in their own journeys toward educational and career goals

Mentor Behaviors

- Offering of personal thoughts and genuine feelings to emphasize value of learning from unsuccessful or difficult experiences (as trial and error and self-correction and not as growth-limiting "failures")
- Selection of related examples from own life (and experiences as mentor of other mentees) based on probable motivational value

- Direct, realistic assessment of positive belief in mentees' abilities to pursue goals
- Confident view of appropriate risk taking as necessary for personal, educational, training, and career development
- Use of statements that clearly encourage personal actions to attain stated objectives

Factor 6: Student Vision

Stimulates mentees' critical thinking with regard to envisioning their own future and to developing their personal and professional potential

Purpose

To encourage mentees as they manage personal changes and take initiatives in their transitions through life events as independent adult learners

Mentor Behaviors

- Statements that require reflection on present and future educational, training, and career attainments
- Questions aimed at clarifying perceptions (positive and negative) about personal ability to manage change
- Review of individual choices based on reasonable assessment of options and resources
- Comments directed at analysis of problem-solving strategies
- Expressions of confidence in carefully thought out decisions
- Remarks that show respect for capacity to determine own future
- Encouragement to develop talents and pursue "dreams"

References

Baskett, H.K.M., Marsick, V. J., and Cervero, R. "Putting Theory to Practice and Practice to Theory." In H.K.M. Baskett and V. J. Marsick (eds.), *Professionals' Ways of Knowing: New Findings on How to Improve Professional Education.* New Directions for Adult and Continuing Education, no. 55. San Francisco: Jossey-Bass, 1992.

Beder, H. "Purposes and Philosophies of Adult Education." In S. B. Merriam and P. M. Cunningham (eds.), *Handbook of Adult and Continuing Education.* San Francisco: Jossey-Bass, 1989.

Brookfield, S. D. *Understanding and Facilitating Adult Learning: A Comprehensive Analysis of Principles and Effective Practices.* San Francisco: Jossey-Bass, 1986.

Civikly, J. M. "Meeting the Challenge." In J. M. Civikly (ed.), *Communicating in College Classrooms.* New Directions for Teaching and Learning, no. 26. San Francisco: Jossey-Bass, 1986.

Cohen, N. H. *The Development and Validation of the Principles of Adult Mentoring Scale for Faculty Mentors in Higher Education.* Dissertation. University Microfilms no. 9316468. Ann Arbor, Mich.: University Microfilms, 1993.

Cohen, N. H. *Mentoring Adult Learners: A Guide for Educators and Trainers.* Malabar, Fla.: Krieger, 1995.

Daloz, L. A. *Effective Teaching and Mentoring: Realizing the Transformational Power of Adult Learning Experiences.* San Francisco: Jossey-Bass, 1986.

Galbraith, M. W. (ed.). *Facilitating Adult Learning: A Transactional Process.* Malabar, Fla.: Krieger, 1991.

Galbraith, M. W., and Zelenak, B. S. "The Education of Adult and Continuing Education Practitioners." In S. B. Merriam and P. M. Cunningham (eds.), *Handbook of Adult and Continuing Education.* San Francisco: Jossey-Bass, 1989.

Holmes, O. W., Jr. In *Bartlett's Familiar Quotations.* (15th ed.) Boston: Little, Brown, 1980.

Hurst, J. C., and Pratt, G. A. "Enhancing Students' Intellectual and Personal Development." In R. B. Winston, Jr., T. K. Miller, S. C. Ender, T. J. Grites, and Associates, *Developmental*

Academic Advising: Addressing Students' Educational, Career, and Personal Needs. San Francisco: Jossey-Bass, 1984.

Knowles, M. S. *The Modern Practice of Adult Education.* New York: Association Press, 1970.

Schlossberg, N. K., Lynch, A. Q., and Chickering, A. W. *Improving Higher Education Environments for Adults.* San Francisco: Jossey-Bass, 1989.

Schön, D. A. *Educating the Reflective Practitioner: Toward a New Design for Teaching and Learning in the Professions.* San Francisco: Jossey-Bass, 1987.

NORMAN H. COHEN *is associate professor of English at the Community College of Philadelphia.*

Institutionally oriented mentoring programs have a positive impact not only on protégés and mentors but also on an organization's ability to retain students or employees.

Organizationally Sponsored Mentoring

Kenneth M. Kerr, Donald R. Schulze, Lyle E. Woodward

One dominant theme found in most organizations is the identification, recruitment, and retention of its members. Any premature turnover in membership, whether the members are students, secretaries, accountants, drivers, mechanics, middle-management team members, support personnel, or even chief executive officers, can have a deleterious effect on the productivity of both the individual and the organization.

Several pragmatic remedies can be cited for this concern about turnover, not the least of which is a mentoring program. In this chapter, the definition of mentoring follows Murray (1991), who calls mentoring the matching of two individuals, one lesser skilled and the other more skilled. The outcome is to have the lesser-skilled person grow and develop specific competence. Such an undertaking, appropriate for almost any organization, can have a significant impact on both recruitment and retention of organizational members.

When we look specifically at institutions of higher education, we see that the rate at which students drop out of colleges and universities has long been a concern to faculty, parents, administrators, and students themselves. Oftentimes, the primary reasons identified by dropouts for their behavior reflect a sense of isolation, lack of adequate preparation prior to arrival at the college, or vagueness of future academic plans and focus. For many minorities and other discrete groups, these reasons are frequently even more pronounced than they are for dropouts overall (Bedient, Snyder, and Simon, 1992; Fleming, 1993; Pantano, 1994).

To combat these student perceptions as they impose themselves on rates of recruitment and retention, a mentoring program should be considered. As Jacobi (1991, p. 505) points out, in the case of education, "mentoring . . . is increasingly looked to today as a retention and enhancement strategy for undergraduate education."

Mentoring Program Design

The first factor in designing a mentoring program, for both academic and other organizations, is verification of the real concerns that the program is to address. What is the student dropout or employee turnover rate? How has it changed recently? Is there a trend or pattern developing? How is the result noticeable? Once documentation has been obtained or defined by the organization's own research processes, then the processes for remediation can take place. These must be agreed upon throughout the organization, particularly at the top level with the president or CEO. Any attempt to implement a mentoring program will be enhanced if the program is visibly endorsed and supported at the highest level. As Scott (1993, p. 347) emphasizes, "Mentoring efforts must be validated from the top down, and seen as a priority throughout the institution."

Once the commitment has been defined, assured, and communicated, the next factor is the identification of the exact population to be mentored, as defined by the earlier research. Realistically, it may be necessary to triage the resources available to those most in need within an organization. Thus, careful analysis of the dropout or turnover rate is necessary in order to expend funds and staff time effectively.

Several studies reflect the appropriateness of mentoring for underrepresented, culturally diverse populations on college and university campuses (Nelson, 1993; Olson and Ashton-Jones, 1992; Pantano, 1994; Taylor, Furcron-Harris, and Ferguson, 1993). Employment opportunities for these categories of individuals would similarly be improved by mentoring in regard to achieving affirmative action and EEOC standards.

After defining the population to be mentored, it is imperative that a clear set of measurable objectives or goals be established against which progress may be measured. In their most generic form, such goals should focus on utilitarian outcomes, as opposed to achievement goals, which may be incorporated later. Students or employees need first to establish a sense of shared interests, space, purposes, and commonality as objectives. They then can more effectively focus on grades, sales, productivity, careers, and so forth. These objectives will help staff clearly define the purposes and parameters of the mentoring program and avoid the problem of imprecision that sometimes affects mentors, protégés, and the mentoring process itself (Jacobi, 1991; Olson and Ashton-Jones, 1992).

The primary but not exclusive purposes of a mentoring program are to give employees or students a support system with a mentor and a connection through that mentor to other campus or organizational resources and networks; to provide peer awareness of others in the mentoring program in order to diminish protégés' sense of isolation; to provide realistic support and feedback regarding protégés' current and future status; to develop greater protégé self-awareness of strengths and abilities; and to provide relationships with caring and concerned mentors, enhancing the linkage of protégés to the organization.

Mentoring Program Implementation

The process of setting up a mentoring program should consider several specific factors in order to ensure both program success and participation in the program.

Selection of Director. Once the support of senior-level personnel has been obtained, attention must next be directed to the choice of a mentoring director. This is a critically important decision since the driving force of this program will be the administrator in charge. Upon selection, this individual will immediately be perceived as the all-knowing expert when it comes to every aspect of mentoring. A more realistic assumption, however, is that many people will need to share the commitment in order for the full effects of the program to evolve. The director is more facilitator than expert, more a mentor to the organization in a larger sense.

Therefore, a person with administrative skills and a firm commitment to the concept of mentoring should be considered. Because this choice may be the single most important factor in the overall success of the program, it should not be considered an add-on appointment. The director must be comfortable with the processes of mentoring and be sensitive to the specific populations to be served. Additional necessary skills include the ability to routinely monitor the program, extend particular attention to the careful selection and matching of mentors and protégés, provide appropriate training and orientation sessions, resolve conflicts between mentors and protégés, identify and secure necessary resources, stay current in his or her own professional development, serve as spokesperson to the organization, and provide ongoing assessment of outcomes.

Selection of Mentors. When an organization decides to initiate a formal mentoring program, it may be prudent to conduct a small pilot program first. In addition, caution must be exhibited when evolving a program so that it does not by title or innuendo appear to be exclusionary. Plans for serving a particular population must include the input of members of that population. A program will have a greater chance of success if the selection criteria for mentors are limited to the skills and qualifications deemed essential to the program's success. A large, highly diverse pool of potential participants, although challenging to screen, will provide the needed range of options for selecting and matching initial mentor-protégé pairs for the pilot program (Phillips-Jones, 1989).

In response to an invitation to serve as a mentor, many people from throughout the entire organization are likely to volunteer. Each respondent should be interviewed by the program director, who will realistically describe the role and responsibilities of mentoring. The director must specify the type and frequency of involvement and reporting that will be required and include an accurate estimate of the time the mentor may be expected to spend and the type of activities he or may be expected to use in developmental functions with the protégé (Murray, 1991).

The actual definition, specifics, and longevity of the mentoring relationship will be determined by the purpose and philosophy of the organization initiating the program. Some relationships may last as briefly as a few months while others may last for several years.

Selection of Protégés. Protégés are approached to participate in many of the same ways mentors are solicited, that is, word of mouth, peer recruitment, and printed material and general announcements distributed to all members of an organization. The benefits of participation as well as the parameters are broadcast, and program staff should note that research shows the most appreciated benefit of the mentoring relationship is the encouragement, the "I know you can do it" support protégés receive, which in turn enhances their own self-confidence and motivation levels (Phillips-Jones, 1989).

Both mentors and protégés are selected based on their individual preferences and availability. Once selected, each receives a profile of his or her protégé or mentor. In all cases, the mentoring relationship should be activated as soon as possible after the participants are paired. Mentor-protégé meeting frequency can range from once per week to once per month, with the details defined by the paired participants.

Orientation and Expectations. Once the pool of participants has been established, the orientation of the mentors and protégés is ready to take place. Invitations need to be sent to each volunteer and to any resource people who may assist during the initial meetings, one for mentors and one for protégés. The orientation meetings "should include an overview of the mentoring program." In addition, "the purpose and process should be reviewed in order to ensure that participants are aware of the goals, [objectives], and activities of the program" (Academic Senate for California Community Colleges, 1993, p. 9). Unrealistic or unclear expectations of the mentoring process on the part of either partner can cause the relationship to become uncomfortable and even fail. Therefore, it is imperative to define what may be anticipated as derivative of the relationship. For example, mentors do not loan money, do protégé homework, violate a confidence, expect to produce a clone of themselves, solve personal problems, or replace a parent. Similar limitations on the part of the protégé must also be defined up front. Without this clarity, trouble can be predicted. These limitations should be shared with both mentors and protégés as each group explores the specific protocols that will govern the relationship. Details surrounding the initial introductory meeting between mentor and protégé are important items to be determined. How the meetings are to be initiated, the where and when of the meetings, how long they will be, and the topics to be discussed are part of the orientation provided by the program director. Throughout each relationship, the program director must be available to assist participants and ensure the success of the relationship. In those rare cases where a participant may wish to be rematched or perhaps to leave the relationship, the director should facilitate the change smoothly, quietly, and without damage to either party. The opportunity for a no-fault termination must be a part of the policy and procedures and should be emphasized during the orientation.

Practical considerations for orientation meetings include written materials and handouts for each group's session, reinforcement of the program objectives, and stimulation of questions during the meeting. In addition, participating mentors "should be made aware of the various [support] services offered. . . . If there is a formal or informal process for referrals, it should be identified in the orientation" (Academic Senate for California Community Colleges, 1993, p. 9). Referral and community resource services that support the mentoring experience should also be detailed. In some cases, it may be prudent to invite resource experts from the relevant referral services to participate. The level of their contributions will be dictated by the structure of the meeting.

The orientation sessions for both mentors and protégés might include an outside consultant if the director is new to a mentoring program. The consultant should be well versed in the philosophy and practice of mentoring programs and provide an overview of such programs. The director gives a brief introduction and is responsible for helping participants reduce their initial anxieties and for coordinating the flow of the group processes. The director can also handle explanations of philosophy, history, and the need for a mentoring program. The consultant deals with the how-to specifics of the structure, issues, and role of mentoring. Each group should also take an extensive look at the anticipated mentoring relationship, including such key issues as the limits of information sharing, the defining and facilitating of the protégé's focus, confrontation skills, role model behaviors, and listening and understanding skills (Cohen, 1995).

For both mentors and protégés, role-playing a simulated initial interview with a protégé or mentor is a worthwhile exercise, allowing participants to become more comfortable with the mentoring concept and to identify potential problem areas for further discussion. The focus in these exercises includes effective listening and other facilitative interview techniques that enhance the mutual relationship between mentor and protégé.

If there are students or employees currently serving as mentors or protégés, their descriptions of their participation may be very helpful, sharing insights and experiences as well as citing cautions and limitations. This sharing will move the orientation sessions from the strictly theoretical to the actual and practical.

If mentoring assignments have not been made before the orientation meetings, it is appropriate to explain how they are made and the criteria used. Participants will then better understand the selection and matching process, and there will be an opportunity for participant feedback and subsequent clarification of the criteria in response. The director should have the assignment process in place before the orientation meeting and perhaps a tentative list of matches drawn up. Based on information shared at the meeting, adjustments may be accommodated before the matches are confirmed.

Last, but certainly not least, there should be a mechanism for evaluation of the orientation sessions. Obtaining a written evaluation from each participant is recommended. The structure of this form may vary from the general to the very specific, depending on the information desired. A well thought out evaluation, however, can be useful when structuring future meetings, when monitoring the progress and motivation of the participants, and in identifying potential problem areas. This document may be an early warning system for the director, one that can make the difference between the success or failure of the program.

Matching Mentor and Protégé. Effective mentors should represent a variety of diverse backgrounds and come from various levels within the organization. The actual matching should be done by considering the characteristics and needs of each individual mentor and protégé. Examples of criteria for matching include career aspirations, gender, ethnicity, interests, availability, or any other special features likely to affect the relationship. This information forms the profiles for the mentors and protégés.

Interest inventories, for example, are available for both mentors and protégés and can be used to make compatible matches. Mentors' and protégés' profile data are also utilized for this task. As mentioned earlier, notification letters to participants should include profiles for each partner in the pair and dates for mentorship program sessions. After the initial matches are determined, a list of alternate mentors and protégés should be generated as a reserve pool to expand the program or serve as replacements. As emphasized by Phillips-Jones (1989, p. 54), "even when you've carefully screened and matched pairs, one or more may not work out. Encourage the pairs to try the relationships for a time and to let you [the director] know of any concerns or desired changes. Quietly make changes, if appropriate, using your pool of alternates (or doubling up on mentors or mentees) if necessary."

Follow-Up Activities. Once a mentoring program has been established, it is critically important that follow-up activities begin immediately. Both mentors and protégés must feel comfortable that the director is a resource to be called upon to address any concerns or questions that might arise. More proactively, however, the director should be in touch with each participant at least every few weeks. Such communications can be as informal as a drop-by visit or telephone call or as formal as a scheduled appointment. Regardless of the form of communication, the emphasis is on the availability of the director's support and his or her approval of the mentoring process underway.

Opportunities for additional social, ongoing training, and skills development sessions should be provided to both mentors and protégés. These sessions can be for individuals or for groups and should reinforce mentoring as a dynamic process with changing roles and parameters. Participants are expected to stay current. Videotapes, lectures, role-playing, modeling, and retreats are some of the ways through which both mentors and protégés can be encouraged to enhance, develop, refresh, or refine their skills.

It is equally important for mentors and protégés to meet collectively on a regular basis, so that each participant gets a sense of the size and importance of the program. This shared activity, perhaps once every two months, allows each participant to meet others who share similar roles. Just as important are separate group meetings for mentors and protégés. Such meetings need to be facilitated by the director of the program. By expanding their networks of peer contacts, mentors and protégés will more clearly realize their unique roles in the larger organization. This reinforcement will strengthen the commitment of each to participate more fully. Stroking and acknowledgment by organization leaders can also be an important part of these events, reflecting the importance of the program.

Program Assessment. There are a number of ways to evaluate a mentoring program. Doing so early can improve pilot program efforts and make implementation of the full program more successful. The organization can continually assess statistical outcomes, achievement of objectives for the organization's target protégé population, and factors such as organizational commitment, costs, training effectiveness, and long-term value. With sound evaluation data, organizational leaders can make objective decisions about repeating, modifying, eliminating, or expanding the program in the future (Phillips-Jones, 1989).

One common form of evaluation consists of asking mentors and protégés to complete questionnaires about their experiences at the end of a specific time frame. Five additional options available for evaluation processes are to develop a comprehensive database for record keeping and program documentation; collect written evaluations at the end of orientation and training sessions; collect informal verbal data and anecdotal records; use participants' journals (with permission) if available; and use mail surveys, telephone interviews, personal interviews, e-mail, or questionnaires or a combination of these methods.

However, as Murray (1991, p. 165) has stated, also keep in mind that "mentoring programs are interactive and nonlinear. In other words, the protégé and the mentor interact, and they in turn influence and are influenced by other components of the organization. Further, these interactions and influences occur in a convoluted if not chaotic manner. Therefore, an assessment can rarely isolate a single factor or simply sum up several factors."

Despite this, evaluations are essential in any organization in order to obtain data influential for decision making. Some of the critical information may be derived from the following questions: Are the goals of the program being met? What is the impact on the organization? Is the program cost effective? What are the future plans of both the program and the sponsoring organization? Have the protégés been affected as anticipated? How do the mentors feel about the program and its procedures? What changes are appropriate to enhance effectiveness? How have changes occurred over time, if at all?

It should not be forgotten, however, that individuals are the primary concern of mentoring, and even if only a few are affected, the program may still be a success (Howard and Grosset, 1992).

Recommendations

There are a number of recommendations that need to be considered in appraising either a new or ongoing mentoring program.

Secure top-down support to help assure the success of any program. If the CEO, for example, serves as a mentor, other members of that organization will more clearly appreciate the commitment to the program.

Stay loose. Flexibility is essential. Time lines and expectations may need to be rethought or revised.

Include all units of an organization in the design and implementation of the program.

Do not assume that mentoring program purposes or processes are widely understood by everyone. Education and communication about a program must both precede the program and continue thereafter.

Be very specific about expectations and limitations. It must be explicitly clear what mentoring is and, equally important, what it is not. Define terms and anticipated outcomes realistically for all participants, including legal, social and ethical parameters.

Provide appropriate support for the program and participants. Whether for financial, technical, or operational support, including professional development, the program will incur costs that it needs to meet as a stand-alone program.

Design a program of ongoing appraisal and assessment. Determine if the mentoring program is serving its intended purpose. Measure the outcomes consistently.

Keep the entire organization informed about the mentoring program on a routine basis. Use statistics and success stories, and a greater level of support will likely come forth from the entire organization.

Consider using part-time employees, faculty, or volunteers as mentors. For example, as Boyden (1994) notes, teachers perform as mentors for most of their professional careers and would be very good at mentoring as volunteers once retired from those careers.

Conclusion

Mentoring programs not only benefit the protégés but also have a positive effect and impact on the mentors and the success of the organization. Hence, mentoring becomes a worthwhile endeavor for any organization to pursue. By addressing the needs of one or more target groups within the institution, mentoring helps the organization meet its goals and objectives, and it encourages contact (and reduces isolation) between experienced and developing members. A successful mentoring program, however, must have endorsement from the top administration down and a commitment to identify a director who has official responsibility for the success of the program. The skills of the director are critical. This individual should be sensitive to the goals and objectives of the organization but must also be able to address the varied needs of all mentor and protégé participants. The relevant tasks will include administering the entire program, facilitating regular meetings, and handling day-to-day problems. The director must also be skillful in utilizing the vast resources of the entire organization's membership and remain flexible to its changing needs.

Mentors and protégés alike have reported that mentoring is a highly satisfying and rewarding experience that fosters a cohesiveness within the organization while encouraging the more complete development of each individual. The extent of the true value of a mentoring program to an organization, as a fluid, dynamic process and not simply as an end result, is often beyond measure.

References

Academic Senate for California Community Colleges. *Student Mentoring: Responding to the Laroche Challenge*. California Community Colleges, 1993. (ED 364 280)

Bedient, D., Snyder, V., and Simon, M. C. "Retirees Mentoring at-Risk College Students." *Phi Delta Kappan*, 1992, 73 (6), 462–470.

Boyden, N. "Retired Teachers Serving as Mentors." In *Proceedings of the International Mentoring Association, U.S.A.* Kalamazoo: Office of Conferences and Institutes, Western Michigan University, 1994.

Cohen, N. H. *Mentoring Adult Learners: A Guide for Educators and Trainers*. Malabar, Fla.: Krieger, 1995.

Fleming, J. "Negotiating College Life." *Black Collegian*, Jan./Feb. 1993, p. 18.

Howard, J., and Grosset, J. "Student Responses to a Community College Faculty Mentoring Program." *Community College Review*, 1992, 20 (1), 48–53.

Jacobi, M. "Mentoring and Undergraduate Academic Success: A Literature Review." *Review of Educational Research*, 1991, 61 (4), 505–532.

Murray, M. *Beyond the Myths and Magic of Mentoring: How to Facilitate an Effective Mentoring Program*. San Francisco: Jossey-Bass, 1991.

Nelson, R. *The Effect of SLS 1122 and Faculty Mentors on Student Performance*. 1993. (ED 371 778).

Olson, G. A., and Ashton-Jones, E. "Doing Gender: (En)gendering Academic Mentoring." *Journal of Education*, 1992, 174 (3), 114–127.

Pantano, J. *Comprehensive Minority SEM Programs at Santa Fe Community College*. 1994. (ED 371 797)

Phillips-Jones, L. *The Mentoring Program Coordinator's Guide*. Grass Valley, Calif.: Coalition of Counseling Centers, 1989.

Scott, S. K. "Academic Mentoring: The Road to Success." In *Proceedings of the International Mentoring Association, U.S.A.* Kalamazoo: Office of Conferences and Institutes, Western Michigan University, 1993.

Taylor, A. Y., Furcron-Harris, R., and Ferguson, B., "Mentoring on a Shoestring." In *Proceedings of the International Mentoring Association, U.S.A.* Kalamazoo: Office of Conferences and Institutes, Western Michigan University, 1993.

KENNETH M. KERR *is dean of students at Ocean County College, Toms River, New Jersey.*

DONALD R. SCHULZE *is director of counseling at Ocean County College.*

LYLE E. WOODWARD *is acting director, Office of Multicultural Services, Ocean County College.*

A study of fifteen mentoring programs and a close examination of the Sponsor-A-Scholar program offer insights into the design and effectiveness of mentoring programs for at-risk young adults, the components of a model program, and comprehensive program evaluations.

Mentoring Program Practices and Effectiveness

Amy W. Johnson, Judith A. Sullivan

Many young adults are growing up and leaving the educational system earlier than their capabilities warrant; they either drop out of high school prior to graduation, or they graduate but do not pursue a college degree despite having the potential to do so. For some, this is a result of isolation from the caring and consistent adult relationships that research has shown to be a common factor among those who achieve success despite disadvantaged circumstances. For others, the cost of higher education stands as an insurmountable obstacle to further educational achievement. And for others still, the lack of information regarding the options and realities of college attendance closes the door to further pursuit of this educational path.

Impatient with public education's failings in these areas, organizations are increasingly trying private interventions in order to stem the tide of failure and unmet potential. Mentoring programs are one such intervention. This chapter investigates two questions: What does the array of mentoring programs that target young adults look like? and, What do we know about these programs' effectiveness? The chapter next discusses the role of the mentor in practice, based upon the experiences of a mentoring program, Sponsor-A-Scholar, and then discusses program evaluation.

Landscape of Mentoring Programs

The current mentoring movement can be described in three ways: there is rampant growth; it is highly decentralized; and there is little available research to help direct practice.

Rampant Growth. There is extensive evidence as to the rampant growth of mentoring programs. Since 1986, when the original I Have a Dream (IHAD)

NEW DIRECTIONS FOR ADULT AND CONTINUING EDUCATION, no. 66, Summer 1995 © Jossey-Bass Inc., Publishers

program was founded by Eugene Lang, an event now viewed as the inspiration for the founding of many other mentoring programs, the IHAD model has spread to over 150 sites (Higgins, Furano, Toso, and Branch, 1991). United Way of America, in partnership with a national organization called One to One, has established One to One operations across the country; these operations provide information kits to interested parties that include materials on how to start your own mentoring program as well as a training curriculum for mentors and mentees. Resource directories of local programs are also available; in Philadelphia alone, the city's Mentoring Institute lists thirty-two local programs (One to One, 1990). There are statewide initiatives in a number of states, including Oregon, New York, New Mexico, Kansas, Minnesota, California, and Rhode Island. In Rhode Island, students are mentored starting as early as the third grade; the state's goal is ultimately to have all children in the state matched with a mentor (Rhode Island Children's Crusade for Higher Education, 1993–1994).

Decentralization. Concurrent with this rampant growth is a highly decentralized array of programs. While there are some statewide efforts, noted above, the vast majority of programs are local efforts with unique designs. The following discussion is based upon fifteen such mentoring programs that were culled from an in-depth review of the literature on mentoring programs; these fifteen were selected based upon their inclusion of a substantive evaluation component. They include programs such as Career Beginnings, which operates in sites throughout the U.S. and Canada; Project LIVE (Collier and Associates, 1992), which operates in New York City; Project RAISE (McPartland and Nettles, 1991), which serves young adults in seven communities in Baltimore; and Adopt-A-Student (Stanwyck and Anson, 1989), which serves students in the Atlanta public school system.

Within this set of fifteen programs, the number of participants ranges from ten per site to all eligible students in a district. The age of the participants served by these mentoring programs also ranges, from as early as first grade to as late as twelfth grade. Most of those served by a mentoring program are "disadvantaged" or "at risk." Using academic indicators, programs tend to focus on students who show classic signs of possible failure but concurrent signs of the potential to succeed. Exactly which signs of possible failure to consider varies from program to program, but many programs focus on school performance or the socioeconomic status of students' families. Some programs dip farther into the at-risk pool than do others and specifically target those who have already failed one or more school subjects.

Program design is largely a function of a program's objectives. Academic objectives are the goal of most mentoring programs, followed by objectives related to attitude, self-esteem, school attendance, and workforce skills. Program components or services provided vary. All of the fifteen programs reviewed offered mentoring as a component, of course. Seven of the fifteen programs, however, offered only the services of a mentor, with no additional support available. Of those programs that did offer additional support, all offered some type of academic support. A variety of other services were also offered, including life skills workshops, an organized summer component, workforce training, and financial support.

Though these are all called mentoring programs, there is a fair amount of program variation in who the mentors are, the duration of the relationship, and the number of mentees for whom each adult is responsible. Mentors are sometimes drawn from within a school, from the ranks of teachers or guidance staff; frequently, they are drawn from the population of adults in the local community, unconnected by any particular tie other than the desire to help; and frequently, they are drawn from a particular business or group of businesses. In the latter case, they usually provided much of the mentoring in the form of work experience.

Evidence from the fifteen programs examined reveals that what constitutes a "sustained" relationship varies tremendously. The duration of participation in a program ranges from several months to seven years, and contact with a mentor ranges from weekly to only several times a year. In addition, the intensity of the relationship varies: some programs ask adult volunteers to take on as many as five mentees, while others have several adults mentoring one person.

Little Available Research. The extent of the decentralization that characterizes the current mentoring movement is partially a result of the movement's third characteristic: extensive practice with little available research evidence to provide insight and direction. Insufficient research evidence on mentoring hampers confidence as to what constitutes the best program design, in terms of how it is operated, who operates it, who volunteers, what services are offered, what will have a significant impact on the participants and what will not, which young adults stand the greatest chance of gaining from such an intervention, and how to get relationships to work. The National Mentoring Institute, staffed by One to One, estimates that "due to ineffective mentoring practices, inefficient organizational practices, or both, only 20 percent of all provider organizations can be considered effective in recruiting, training, mobilizing and supporting mentoring relationships" (One to One, 1990, p. 4). What does the available evidence suggest?

Is Mentoring Effective?

The rampant growth of mentoring programs, the expectations that accompany the intervention strategy, and the high costs in both dollars and personal resources, combine to make a response to the question of mentoring's effectiveness all the more critical. There are, however, several obstacles to reaching a definitive answer as to whether or not mentoring programs are effective. The first is that there simply are not many well-designed evaluations from which to draw conclusions. The bulk of the evaluation research focuses on input measures such as the number of students mentored, the average length of a relationship, and the number of mentors trained, rather than on outcome measures such as high school performance or college enrollment. Sophisticated program evaluation is an expensive endeavor to undertake; most programs do not have the extra funds to support a research project and, instead, funnel all resources back into program operation.

A second obstacle to answering the question of mentoring's effectiveness is that it is difficult to isolate and attribute outcomes to the mentoring component. Students receive many services both within and outside a mentoring program. Even in the best evaluation designs, with randomly assigned experimental and comparison group students, it is still difficult to control for all relationships and interventions.

A third obstacle to determining if mentoring programs are effective, and one expressed in particular by mentors, is that mentoring could have an important impact many years down the road in a way not yet foreseen by researchers and not detected one or two years after program participation. Many mentors, like parents, believe, or hope, that some of what they say to those they are mentoring will be heard, if not at present then sometime in the future when an important decision has to be made. Most evaluations do not capture this long-term potential outcome.

While mentoring programs are certainly effective at exposing participants to people, places, opportunities, and situations to which they might not normally be exposed, the salient question is whether they are effective at achieving their stated objectives.

Evaluation Findings. Ten of the fifteen programs had findings from quantitative evaluations that measured specific program objectives: either academic, personal, or workforce objectives. In some cases, objectives could not be measured at the time of the evaluation (for example, students were not yet old enough). In other cases, certain objectives were simply not measured. And in yet other cases, a study found mixed results; for example, a positive result for college attendance at one type of institution but a negative result for attendance at another type of institution. Moreover, because the following summary of findings is drawn from a diverse set of programs, populations, and research designs, it is important to exercise caution in saying anything too definitive about the tally of results.

That said, almost 30 percent of all the findings were positive; whether these are outcomes that will be sustained for participants over time is unknown. Over 60 percent of the findings were not significant; whether these findings are not significant in the short term but will evolve into long-term positive outcomes is unknown. About 10 percent of the outcomes were negative, suggesting a particularly cautionary note to concluding that mentoring by mere definition alone is going to be a good thing. Thus, the collection of results—the best of the available evidence on this intervention strategy—does not provide overwhelming support to mentoring's effectiveness.

In looking at the summary of quantitative findings, rather than findings in the aggregate, for each program, the following results emerge. For four out of the ten programs, there were only nonsignificant or negative findings; for two out of the ten, there were both positive and negative outcomes; and for the remaining four out of the ten, there were positive outcomes in conjunction with nonsignificant outcomes.

Do these last four programs, which had positive findings and no negative findings, share certain characteristics (Aiello, 1988; McPartland and Nettles, 1991; Stanwyck and Anson, 1989; Tierney and Branch, 1992)? Three of the four share several characteristics. All three offered academic support in addition to mentoring, suggesting that mentoring may be more effective when combined with other support services. For all three, mentoring was provided by individuals outside of the schools, and for all three the mentor-mentee ratio was 1:1. In two of the three, mentoring was specifically provided at least once per week.

Where does this leave us? One conclusion is that the success of mentoring programs is, not surprisingly, largely a function of who participates and how a program is operated. Some mentoring programs work; others do not. Some are well managed; others are not. Some deliver first-rate training to their mentors; others do not. Some carefully screen potential mentors; others do not. Some available evidence on both quality of relationships and program management gives us insight into the impact of differences in these variables.

Quality of Relationships. The quality of the mentor-mentee relationship is certainly a determinant of outcomes. Research conducted by Public/Private Ventures has looked closely at what makes for a successful relationship between two individuals and has found certain characteristics common to those relationships that were deemed successful: sustained matches were those in which the adults were consistent in meeting with the mentees; in which the adults closely followed the mentees' interests; in which adults reassured the mentees of their value; in which adults often played an instrumental role in helping the mentees cope with some difficult situation; in which adults provided advice that the mentees valued; and in which adults had some contact with the mentees' families (Mecartney, Styles, and Morrow, 1994).

Three of the evaluations being described here included analyses of students who were determined to have been "effectively" or "successfully" mentored versus those for whom mentoring was not successful (Flaherty, 1985; Slicker and Palmer, 1993; Stanwyck and Anson, 1989). In these cases, the researchers clearly recognized that all mentoring is not alike. Flaherty (1985) found that those who were "definitely" mentored, while they too declined in academic performance, declined less than did those who were "somewhat" mentored or not mentored (the experimental students). Slicker and Palmer (1993) found that those students who were "effectively" mentored were less likely to drop out, and improvement in academic achievement for this group approached significance. A more disturbing finding of theirs, however, was that the ineffectively mentored group experienced a significant decline in self-concept when compared to the students who were not mentored at all. In other words, while good mentoring might be beneficial, poor mentoring might be very detrimental. Stanwyck and Anson (1989) found an encouraging outcome for those whose relationships with their mentors were rated as more effective: these students had significantly higher employment rates than did those who did not have such successful relationships with their mentors.

Program Management. Program management or operation is also a possible determinant of outcomes. Both McPartland and Nettles (1991) and Cave and Quint (1990) analyzed data across multiple sites—seven in both cases. Each study found that some outcomes were significant at certain sites but not at others, clearly indicating that program implementation plays a very large role in the effectiveness of the intervention. Results from McPartland and Nettles' study found that one site that had significant and positive student outcomes did not yet have a mentoring component in operation, while another site that had a fully operational mentoring component had no significant outcomes.

Clearly, there is a need to continue evaluation research. A good evaluation can address such critical issues as whether a program is successful in achieving its stated objectives, which young adults are benefiting, and whether certain adults or mentoring behaviors are more effective than others. Mentoring programs have the potential to make significant contributions in the social policy and education arenas should they prove to make a difference in the lives of disadvantaged young adults.

Sponsor-A-Scholar

This section provides insight into the kinds of operational issues that must be considered and monitored throughout the life of a program. The analysis draws on the experiences of the Sponsor-A-Scholar program. It is followed by a discussion of program evaluation, again using the current longitudinal evaluation being conducted of the Sponsor-A-Scholar program as an example of what critical components need to be included in a meaningful study.

Program Design. Philadelphia Futures' Sponsor-A-Scholar program originated five years ago, as one of the aforementioned variations on Eugene Lang's I Have A Dream model. (Philadelphia Futures is a nonprofit organization dedicated to motivating youths to stay in school and prepare for college and career opportunities.) Individuals, corporations, or other organizations sponsor one student for college by creating a "last dollar" scholarship and by mentoring the student from ninth grade through freshman year of college. Additionally, the Sponsor-A-Scholar program provides extensive program support, college counseling and preparation, and academic enrichment and support throughout the duration of the five-year commitment.

The students in the Sponsor-A-Scholar program are drawn from Philadelphia's comprehensive high schools, where college preparatory resources are fewer than in the magnet high schools. College counseling is quite limited, and the dropout rates in some comprehensive high schools exceed 50 percent ("A District in Distress," 1994, p. G4). Students accepted into the program are recommended by their eighth-grade guidance counselors on the basis of good grades, motivation to attend college, ability to relate to an adult in a long-term relationship, and the agreement of a parent or guardian who is supportive of the program goals. Students must also meet the program's financial eligibility guidelines.

The mentors in the program are a diverse group and come from a wide variety of backgrounds and professions. One-half live in the city, and one-half live in the suburbs. Sixty percent of the mentors are between the ages of thirty and fifty, one-third are more than fifty years old, and 7 percent are under thirty. Regardless of their age, new mentors sometimes ask with some trepidation if they will need knowledge or skills beyond what they receive during their regular mentor training and subsequent support sessions with other mentors and staff. Many mentors have little specific knowledge of urban education; few are social workers; and fewer have firsthand experience of what growing up in the inner city is like for a teenager today. Without this experience, they wonder, what qualifies them to mentor a young person? Do their attitudes and willingness to help predispose them to becoming successful mentors? Are there "natural instincts" (Mahoney, 1983, p. 10) or positive characteristics of a skilled mentor that may be identified and developed in well-meaning individuals?

Training and Development of a Skilled Mentor. Clearly, instincts of compassion, concern, and goodwill alone do not prepare prospective mentors to participate with adolescents whose life experiences are very different from their own. The Sponsor-A-Scholar program, therefore, provides extensive support and training for mentors to assist them in helping an economically disadvantaged, academically promising young person to achieve his or her potential, to graduate from high school, and to complete college successfully. Each mentor participates in an orientation session that provides information and context about the program goals, activities, and expectations; issues affecting inner-city youths and urban education; and strategies for successful mentoring. These sessions usually occur in a group setting, and prospective mentors are encouraged to ask questions and share their fears and concerns. Frequently, an experienced mentor is present to share firsthand information and experience.

Each group of thirty to thirty-five students in Sponsor-A-Scholar is shepherded by a coordinator who is in contact at least once each month with both the student and the mentor. The coordinator assures that mentors and students are meeting regularly and that their relationship is developing in support of the student's needs and goals. The coordinator monitors the student's academic progress, acts as a liaison with school personnel, and provides students and mentors with information about program activities and opportunities, identifying other enrichment resources for the students. The coordinator is the primary link to the program for both mentors and students, the "glue in the mentoring process" (Freedman, 1993, p. 100), and an integral part of program design and success.

Patterns of interaction between mentors and students are often established within the first year. Consequently, coordinators monitor new relationships very closely. After three months, and sometimes again after six months, mentors and students meet with their coordinator to review their progress and the program's goals and expectations. The coordinator may work with the students and mentors separately and together to clarify any misunderstanding and to suggest and to develop alternative approaches that are compatible with the personalities of both the mentor and the student. In addition, the coordinator encourages both members in the relationship to relax and to be themselves. In effect, the coordinator works to hone the "natural instincts" of the well-intentioned mentor by providing information and feedback to develop new skills in the mentor. In the few cases where a clear incompatibility arises, mentors and students may be reassigned.

Programmatic support for mentors also includes regularly scheduled mentor roundtable debriefing sessions, opportunities for mentors to meet and talk informally about their relationships with their students, and lectures and seminars from experts in fields such as mentoring, adolescent development, college selection and preparation, multicultural diversity, and alternative English. Coordinators often schedule individual appointments with mentors and students, which sometimes include parents and school personnel. Support is highly individualized, depending upon the needs and personalities of a given pair and the circumstances. The Sponsor-A-Scholar program works to prepare and train the mentor to become skillful and to be the critical agent of change, growth, and ultimately, academic and social success through his or her relationship with the student.

Responsibilities and Practices of a Skilled Mentor. The Sponsor-A-Scholar program calls for the adult to mentor the student through the difficult transition from middle school to a much larger urban high school, and then from high school to college. The mentor's primary job—the goal of Sponsor-A-Scholar—is to assist the student in staying focused on completing high school and going on to college by providing encouragement and by helping the student to realize his or her potential.

Experience in the Sponsor-A-Scholar program has shown that the most successful mentors are those who are willing to reflect on their roles and on their own expectations, biases, and limitations. As part of the ongoing training and support that the program provides, staff coordinators tactfully challenge and encourage mentors to engage in this kind of reflection. Further, coordinators may gently make mentors aware of unconscious assumptions and biases that are hindering the development of their relationship with their students. Through the benefit of this self-knowledge, mentors are then better positioned to understand the dynamics of their relationships with their students, to extend themselves beyond the confines of their own experiences to understand a young person, and to overcome the gulfs of age, race, class, and culture that often separate them from the students they are seeking to help.

When mentors are able to put aside their own ambitions, hopes, and fears and see the often inchoate ambitions, hopes, and fears of their younger partners, they are able to develop a mentoring relationship built on a framework that is supportive of the students' innate talents and abilities while still guiding the students toward new knowledge and experience. As Marc Freedman

(1993, p. 101) observes, "Mentors who enter the relationship with preconceived ideas about what the areas of focus will be, the ways in which they will help young adults, and the subjects to be discussed frequently find themselves facing a brick wall." The art of successful mentoring lies in establishing this special and delicate balance in a relationship with a developing adolescent who is constantly changing, testing, growing, and unfolding over a five-year period.

To achieve this youth-centered balance requires maturity, patience, perseverance, the ability to listen actively and without judgment, and the awareness that while the mentoring relationship has its unique characteristics, it is in many important ways like every other relationship in the mentor's and student's lives. Mentoring relationships, like all other relationships, have ups and downs—intense periods and times of withdrawal and distraction. Mentors who understand the flux of their interactions with their students in this context and who are able to resist their own temporary feelings of personal rejection, feelings of discouragement, and need for fast results have a great advantage in building meaningful relationships.

Mentoring goals of cultivating a students' talents and dreams with new information, opportunity, and experience are seldom achieved by mentors who do not communicate clearly, honestly, and constructively and do not demonstrate a respect and sensitivity for differences among individuals. As clearly as a mentor may communicate his or her own role, values, and desire to help a student, however, relationships take time to evolve and adolescents cannot be rushed in this area. Asking too many direct or highly personal questions about family and friends too soon may have the effect of precluding any further disclosure.

Skilled mentors wait for students to share information about themselves when they feel ready. They also look for the subtle cues that their students may give as to how the relationship is developing and what direction it may take overall. When they begin meeting their students, skilled mentors use the time that they spend together for getting to know each other, having fun, and discovering shared or new interests. Relationships work best when students and mentors decide together what their activities will be. Jointly planned meetings offer the opportunity for real fun, spontaneous sharing, and the mutual discovery of new interests. Mentors who develop itineraries on their own and control the conversation to fit their message will not succeed and will also miss an opportunity for personal growth and expanded knowledge and experience.

Even when mentors approach their students with openness and a willingness to listen and follow the student's lead, differences in experience and styles of communication may be troublesome. The staff coordinator plays the important role of helping to bridge these gaps by listening to the concerns of both students and mentors and by constructively reinterpreting, as necessary, the language, actions, or attitudes of one partner in the relationship to the other in order to facilitate better understanding and communication.

Students may place their mentors on pedestals because of their greater experience, information, and resources and may incorrectly believe that mentors cannot understand the challenges, questions, or difficulties that the students may face. To students, mentors' lives may appear so directed and successful that students may naïvely assume that there have been no obstacles. In the interest of improving their relationships and of helping students to succeed, successful mentors share information about their own struggles as well as discuss the value of hard work, determination, and discipline. Specifically, mentors must help students to understand the connections between graduating from high school, doing well in college, and a meaningful career. These conversations give students insight into the fact that success is not a matter of luck and that they have the power and responsibility to influence their own destinies.

Teaching students how to exercise this power and responsibility to fulfill their potential is perhaps the most valuable lesson a mentor can give. Encouraging students to identify opportunities for themselves and to develop problem-solving and coping skills so that they are able to take full advantage of those opportunities is the focus of this instruction. It is accomplished by talking through situations with students, asking questions without providing answers, challenging assumptions and fears, suggesting alternatives that may never have been considered, and providing information and support. A skilled mentor utilizes these tools to help students learn to take responsibility for themselves and to feel hopeful about their futures.

The activity of professionally mentoring a student is complex. The work is sometimes difficult, and the rewards are not always immediately apparent. The process, though, offers the potential for discovery, joy, humor, and growth for both students and mentors, the potential to hand "another along until the moment that allows both of them together to envision possibilities hitherto out of sight" (Coles, 1993, p. 114).

Program Evaluation

How can we know if a mentoring program is effective? How will we know if programs such as Sponsor-A-Scholar are making a significant difference in the lives of those who participate? How will we know if the funds currently allocated to program operation are being spent in the most cost-effective way?

It is critical that programs such as Sponsor-A-Scholar be evaluated in a way that is meaningful. Several aspects in the design of an evaluation and the analysis of data are critical to uncovering results that will advance our knowledge concerning effective interventions for specific populations. First, a comparison group must be identified. In the absence of a comparison group, it would be impossible to rule out the conclusion that those students who succeed after participating in a program such as Sponsor-A-Scholar would have done so anyway, regardless of participation. Second, in order to determine whether participation in a mentoring program is having a significant impact on any of several outcomes, data must be analyzed using multiple regression. Because many of the independent variables are likely to be related to one another or likely to contribute to the outcomes achieved, multiple regression is particularly important in order to introduce some measure of control. Third, an evaluation should provide as longitudinal an assessment of impact as is possible. Those evaluations that look at outcomes immediately following participation risk reporting only short-term impacts that may not be sustained for any length of time. Fourth, and lastly, an evaluation should use attainment of concrete objectives—such as high school performance or college enrollment—as the measure of program success. A focus on input variables—those primarily concerned with program operation, such as the number of young adults mentored—is important but not sufficient to a determination of program effectiveness. A meaningful evaluation should be able to respond directly to the goals of a program: if a program is designed to improve high school attendance, then an evaluation should be able to answer whether high school attendance significantly improved for those who participated in the program.

The evaluation of the Sponsor-A-Scholar program is a longitudinal evaluation now in its second of three years of collection of data for program participants and a comparison group. It is designed to test whether or not the program is effective in its goals of helping Sponsor-A-Scholar students complete high school and attend and remain in college at significantly higher rates than their nonprogram counterparts. Outcomes that will be examined are college enrollment, performance, and retention, high school performance, involvement in college preparation activities, and measures of self-esteem. In addition, specific mentor, student, and school characteristics will be examined in an effort to understand why certain students may do better on the various outcome measures, possibly regardless of program participation. This is a critical component of the analysis and is designed to help in the process of identifying which students stand to gain the most from the available resources. If, for example, a mentoring program is providing services and funds to students who will do well even in the absence of the intervention, then these resources are not being spent in the most cost-effective way.

Data for the evaluation are being collected from students' school records for each year, beginning in ninth grade; from junior high school test scores; from annual surveys of students and a single survey of their mentors; from school district data that contain demographic and other information on the characteristics of each school; and from records kept by the coordinators of each group of Sponsor-A-Scholar students.

Survey data available at the time of this writing—from the first year in which they have been collected—permit a preliminary examination of some important input variables, variables primarily concerned with program operation but not yet related to program outcomes. This type of preliminary examination provides some valuable direction to ongoing program management, but is only suggestive of some areas in which Sponsor-A-Scholar may ultimately witness significant positive outcomes.

Of the 154 Sponsor-A-Scholar students who completed surveys during the academic year 1993–94, almost all are generally very positive about the quality of their relationships and the nature of the interactions with their mentors. Most students, however, would like more contact and an even closer relationship with their mentors. There are noticeable differences in the number of times that students have been to a mentor's home, with about equal numbers saying they have never been to their mentor's home, have been once, have been two or three times, or have been more than three times. None of the mentors regrets being involved, and 70 percent feel that they are making a difference in the lives of the students they mentor. About half of the mentors feel that they needed training to become a mentor; however, only 16 percent feel that the training received was very effective, and 43 percent feel that it was somewhat effective.

Across the board, in every category asked about their relationship, mentors' responses were less positive than were students' responses to the same questions. Mentors are less likely than students to say that they often discuss important things, that they often do enjoyable things, that they are often excited to get together. Mentors are more likely than students to say that they sometimes wish they were in a different mentor/student relationship and that they do not understand their student. They are less likely than students to say that the other person in the relationship respects them a lot, that they have a very close relationship, that they want a closer relationship, and that they want more contact.

When the Sponsor-A-Scholar students are compared to their nonparticipating counterparts, the Sponsor-A-Scholar students are more likely than nonparticipants to say that they will apply to more than one college and less likely to say that they are not going to college at all after high school. In addition, Sponsor-A-Scholar participants are more likely to have taken part in various college preparation activities, such as enrollment in college prep courses, enrollment in an SAT/PSAT prep course, contact with colleges for information, discussion with guidance counselors about options for college, and visits or interviews at colleges.

While this preliminary examination is informative and suggestive, it is not yet based on a full regression analysis with all of the available data. Whether any current differences will be sustained over time, or translate into more substantive differences, such as actual college enrollment, is not yet known. Once the full analysis has been done, however, results from this evaluation should greatly contribute to our knowledge concerning effective interventions with this population.

Conclusion

The evidence on practice and effectiveness available from programs around the country as well as from the experiences to date of the Sponsor-A-Scholar program leads to several conclusions. The first is that there is currently little certainty as to what constitutes best practice in mentoring young adults. The diversity in such program features as the duration of the intervention or relationship, the appropriate mentor/mentee ratio, which adults are sought as mentors, and which students are thought to stand to gain the most is evidence of our lack of certainty. Differences in program design are largely based on local circumstances rather than on knowledge about what works and what does not.

The second conclusion is that mentoring someone—a young adult, perhaps, in particular—is a complex task and not to be underestimated. Meeting with someone periodically and calling someone on the telephone are not such complex tasks, but really mentoring people to the point where they "envision," believe in, seek, and realize "possibilities hitherto out of sight" (Coles, 1993, p. 114) takes a set of difficult skills that run the gamut from patience and perseverance to openness and self-reflection. Programs that assume that mentoring, in the truest sense of the word, will take place absent training and programmatic support of mentors and in a relatively short period of time—in less than two years or so—are probably not going to have much impact, either immediate or sustained.

The third conclusion is that for many programs, the inputs are disproportionately small if the outcomes sought are to be realized. The original design and subsequent experiences of Sponsor-A-Scholar have resulted in a program that provides students and mentors with a whole range of support services. For the mentors, these include training, periodic debriefing sessions with other mentors and program staff, and the support and guidance of the coordinator. For students, these include, in addition to five years of regular contact with a mentor, academic support in the form of tutoring, workshops that focus on the college application process and life skills, college trips, cultural events, class meetings, a newsletter, summer opportunities, and the encouragement and discipline provided by the class coordinator. Programs that seek to make real changes in the personal and academic lives of young adults but that do not provide adequate programmatic inputs to achieve their goals are unlikely to succeed at best and may be detrimental at worst. It is not surprising that a program that provides mentoring for one academic year (ten months), that provides mentoring by school staff already burdened with the responsibilities of dozens of students, and that has a 1:2 mentor to student ratio does not demonstrate positive outcomes in its goals of improved academic performance, attitude toward classes, and attendance (Flaherty, 1985).

Program design and management must focus on the inputs, on the range and extent of services provided to support mentors in their work with young adults. Lack of attention to whether or not a program design is adequately supportive of the outcomes sought destines a program to being ineffective. Conversely, evaluations must focus on the outcomes, on whether a program is achieving its stated goals rather than on reporting the state of the inputs.

Mentoring, as an intervention designed to address the needs and gaps in the lives of many of today's young adults, has the potential to make a real difference for participants. Many interventions to date have failed this population. Careful attention to program design and to effectiveness in achieving program goals is a critical first step in providing adequate and appropriate services and in furthering our knowledge as to how best to serve today's young adults.

References

Aiello, H. S. "Assessment of a Mentor Program on Self-Concept and Achievement Variables of Middle School Underachievers." Unpublished doctoral dissertation, Virginia Polytechnic Institute and State University, 1988.

Cave, G., and Quint, J. *Career Beginnings Impact Evaluation: Findings from a Program for Disadvantaged High School Students.* New York: Manpower Demonstration Research Corporation, 1990.

Coles, R. *The Call of Service.* Boston: Houghton Mifflin, 1993.

Collier, W. V., and Associates. *Saving Youth and Dollars: Project LIVE. A Follow-up Research Study.* New York: Walter V. Collier and Associates, 1992.

"A District in Distress." *Philadelphia Inquirer,* Oct. 23, 1994, p. G4.

Flaherty, B. P. "An Experiment in Mentoring High School Students Assigned to Basic Courses." Unpublished doctoral dissertation, Boston University, 1985.

Freedman, M. *The Kindness of Strangers: Adult Mentors, Urban Youth, and the New Volunteerism.* San Francisco: Jossey-Bass, 1993.

Higgins, C., Furano, K., Toso, C., and Branch, A. *I Have a Dream, in Washington, D.C.* Philadelphia: Public/Private Ventures, 1991.

McPartland, J. M., and Nettles, S. M. "Using Community Adults as Advocates or Mentors for at-Risk Middle School Students: A Two-Year Evaluation of Project RAISE." *American Journal of Education,* 1991, 99 (4), 568–586.

Mahoney, M. "Mentors." In the Annual Report of the Commonwealth Fund. New York: Commonwealth Fund, 1983.

Mecartney, C. A., Styles, M. B., and Morrow, K. V. *Mentoring in the Juvenile Justice System: Findings from Two Pilot Programs.* Philadelphia: Public/Private Ventures, 1994.

One to One. *Mentoring Kit.* Washington, D.C.: One to One, 1990.

Rhode Island Children's Crusade for Higher Education. *1993–94 Fact Sheet* and informational materials. Providence: Rhode Island Children's Crusade for Higher Education, 1993–1994.

Slicker, E. K., and Palmer, D. J. "Mentoring at-Risk High School Students: Evaluation of a School-Based Program." *School Counselor,* 1993, 40, 327–334.

Stanwyck, D. A., and Anson, C. A. *The Adopt-A-Student Evaluation Project. Final Report.* Atlanta: Department of Educational Foundations, Georgia State University, 1989.

Tierney, J. P., and Branch, A. Y. *College Students as Mentors for at-Risk Youth. A Study of Six Campus Partners in Learning Programs.* Philadelphia: Public/Private Ventures, 1992.

AMY W. JOHNSON *is project manager at the Institute for Research on Higher Education, University of Pennsylvania, and principal investigator of the Sponsor-A-Scholar program evaluation.*

JUDITH A. SULLIVAN *is director of the Sponsor-A-Scholar program, run by Philadelphia Futures.*

There are primary developmental benefits of mentoring for adult learners, and the contribution of the mentoring model can be illustrated through practical examples.

The Benefits of Mentoring

Susan F. Schulz

Adult learning, growth, and development can be thought of in terms of change, that is, in terms of the way individuals handle developmental tasks and move from one life stage to the next (Boucouvalas and Krupp, 1989). Learning is a transformational journey that involves relating to other people in some kind of organizational setting. In adult learning, the facilitator has an important role of collaborating with the learner (Brookfield, 1989) so that the learner can use new ways of thinking and acting in order to make changes and handle life's tasks. A mentor can act as such a facilitator, assisting adult learners in working through the different phases of their work and psychosocial lives. A mentoring relationship provides collaborative and experiential learning and may possibly be one of the most developmentally important relationships a person can experience in adulthood (Bova, 1987).

The mentoring relationship benefits both the mentor and the mentee, or protégé. There are subsequent benefits to the mentoring organization and to society as a whole. The relationship between mentor and mentee becomes co-creative because adults experience similar life tasks that can be similarly resolved or addressed. In the mentoring relationship, both parties have the opportunity to move to the next life stage through their mentoring roles.

Erikson (1968) and Levinson and others (1978) each set forth a theory of adult change and development that relates to mentoring. Erikson defines eight levels in his *Stages of Psychosocial Development*. He explains that there are crises that occur periodically throughout life. As adults find solutions to these crises, they are then able to move successfully to the next stage. Levinson used the notion of "life structures" (or roles) in his theory of adult development. There are periods of stability and periods of transition, both with demands on work, family, and personal relationship roles. Like Erikson, Levinson sees each developmental role as having its own tasks. Other adult development theories also assume that there is some order and commonality in the life-cycle. Adults move through a predictable series of stages when there are *teachable moments,* that is, a readiness to learn, such as the time of marriage or of starting a job. Having to deal with individual or cultural life events also provides adults with a way to learn. Life transitions like leaving home, the birth of a child, or loss of parents enable people to learn by developing coping skills. A mentoring relationship can provide opportunities for both the mentor and mentee to learn, grow, and develop at these critical life stages. Mentoring facilitates the transition to the next phase of personal development, mutually benefiting mentor and mentee.

Benefits to the Mentor

For there to be a mentoring relationship, there must be a shared initiative and the willingness of both people to invest their time, energy, emotions, and themselves. Two people have to agree to work together. It should not be surprising that the results would be shared personal enhancement, growth, and satisfaction, as well as improved communication skills. For example, in a faculty peer mentoring program in a community college (Harnish and Wild, 1993), faculty mentors were teamed with faculty mentees. Both parties in the mentor pairs experienced learning and change, with instructional improvement and camaraderie as an outcome. In a peer coaching program in teacher education (Neubert and Stover, 1994), teacher-coaches learned skills and strategies, promoted personal reflection, and developed a sense of collegiality. In mentoring each other, teachers become teacher-learners, which set the tone for continued collaboration.

In her discussion of the phases of the mentor relationship, Kram (1983) points out that the careers and psychosocial development of both participants are enhanced by mentoring. The young person in the initial stages of personal and work life faces a need for role identity and closeness. The protégé benefits from a mentor who focuses on the protégé's career and offers coaching, protection, and challenging work. Mentors are usually older and in midcareer. They are often at a point in life when they are reviewing what they have accomplished and are eager to share their wisdom. As mentors, they gain recognition, respect, and satisfaction by contributing to the younger person. Mentoring clearly benefits both people in the relationship. There is a confirmation of self-worth and acceptance as a result of the interaction.

Learning. In addition to the benefits just described, which both participants gain from the mentoring relationship, the mentor has the opportunity to learn specific skills and new ideas. Mentoring is often part of the induction process in K-12 work settings (Heller and Sindelar, 1991), as new teachers are paired with mentors who are experienced faculty members. Mentors learn new ideas, theories, and ways to teach from these new teachers who have just acquired the latest techniques from university classrooms. Since many experienced teachers have been away from formal classes for a time, mentoring gives them an opportunity to strengthen their subject matter areas as well. The mentor-teachers can also learn more about the art and science of teaching through the self-examination and introspection that often come from coaching someone else. They also have the opportunity to learn or enhance leadership and coaching skills. Mentors benefit from feedback by seeing how mentees put suggested teaching skills and ideas in place. When placed in the position of having to answer questions and help solve problems, they must think critically about themselves and their techniques and seek additional information. In a sense, mentors are both teachers and students.

Growth. The mentor has the opportunity to grow personally and professionally from the mentoring relationship. In coaching someone new to the organization, mentors become aware of their own level of competence. This self-discovery and personal awareness can lead to personal and professional satisfaction and infuse a sense of motivation and revitalized interest into a long-held job. When a mentee asks questions, mentors are forced to open their eyes about what they are doing, reexamine their own performance and decision-making abilities, and evaluate how they got to where they are. Teachers who mentor new teachers may become reacquainted with their own love of teaching. They grow by allowing someone to ask questions and disturb their established routines.

Mentoring can speed advancement within an organization and develop the mentor's reputation as a leader and an expert with knowledge and wisdom to share (Burruss, 1988; Kram, 1983). A protégé can help with work assignments and integrate new ideas into established ways of doing things, with the additional benefit of giving the mentor time to pursue other responsibilities within the organization. Mentors can benefit from increased recognition and visibility, which can open doors to promotions. Mentors' support networks can grow when they introduce their protégés to various contacts within the organization and when their protégés succeed. This sets a tone of collegiality and cooperation, particularly when the work environment has been competitive rather than collaborative.

Development. A mentoring relationship provides the opportunity to progress along each life stage. The successful mentor helps the protégé to understand and experience intimacy, a challenge in early adulthood, through a shared, committed, and close relationship with that protégé. The mentoring relationship offers a way for mentors to face their future in middle adult life, a stage Erikson describes as the dilemma of "generativity vs. stagnation" (1968, p. 138).

Mentors are often older and more mature than their protégés, having reached middle or senior level in their organizations. The question of how they can be of continued value in the work setting can be an overriding concern to them. How to maintain their self-worth when they are closer to the end of a career than the beginning is challenging for most. In a mentoring relationship, professionals can experience the intrinsic value of helping others work toward their goals. They discover they want to make a contribution to a younger person and to their organization.

Mentoring fits into their mature career stage for many mentors because the relationship helps to renew meaning in their lives (Bova, 1987; Kram, 1983). Rejuvenated and reflective describe how mentors feel as they seek to make a significant contribution to society and establish a new role for themselves. Mentors work with juniors and help to ensure that the younger person has the capabilities to be of value to the organization. In addition, they can leave a legacy by empowering the next generation and fostering a new level of management and competent workers.

The mentoring relationship is a way to blend the mentor's past experience and wisdom and bring it forward into the future, a challenge in the mature adult phase. It allows the mentor to achieve a sense of accomplishment by influencing the next generation. Continued personal and professional development at the mature career life stage may hinge on the ability to use relationships with younger protégés to move on. Without some way to make a meaningful contribution to society, mature adults experience stagnation and loss.

Benefits to the Mentee

Like the mentor, the mentee, or protégé, has the opportunity to learn, grow, and to move along life's professional and psychosocial pathways. The literature on outcomes for mentees that result from the mentoring relationship suggests that because life stages and career phases are similar for mentors and mentees, they share some similar benefits. There is a synergism to the mentoring relationship.

Learning. Studies of mentoring relationships occur in many settings and are frequently carried out in schools, colleges, libraries, and business environments (Bova, 1987; Burruss, 1988; Ganser, 1992; Kram, 1983; Selke and Wong, 1993). Learning occurs because the mentor is a one-to-one private tutor. The mentor provides information and the opportunity to practice, role-play, and create strategies. The protégé's work products can be reviewed by the mentor before they are submitted to someone else. The mentor can play devil's advocate, enabling the protégé to experiment with ideas and make changes as needed, all with minimal or reduced risk.

When new teachers are paired with experienced teachers in schools, they quickly learn the formal and informal regulations and procedures in their school. Mentors provide beginning teachers with a customized cram course on the school culture, classroom management, dealing with parents, and working with fellow teachers. Mentees speed past learning basic routines and get on to the job of teaching. They enjoy a fast linkup between what was learned in the classroom and what is needed in the workplace.

Gaining job information that may not otherwise be available (or that may be hard to find) and gaining it quickly is a distinct advantage to the mentee. In a business environment, mentees can learn by being coached and counseled, introduced to the right people, given challenging work assignments, and invited to meetings. They gain access to knowledge about what it takes to be a good performer and learn by being pushed by their mentors to go beyond their own expectations. Mentored new hires learn more about the new job setting than those who rely on co-workers (Ostroff and Koslowski, 1993). They have more knowledge about the technical and organizational workings of the business than fellow workers with no mentor.

When students are paired with faculty in colleges and universities, they have access to information to make better choices in course selection and goal setting. They are aware of program services and can successfully learn how the system works (Mendoza and Samuels, 1987). The knowledge and information provided by the mentor positively affects the student's ability to adjust to the college environment. This is particularly true for individuals at risk, such as first-generation and minority students. Often, these students lack information about academic goals and how to get through the school bureaucracy. Many are unable to cope because of frustration, rejection, or feelings of isolation from their own or a new culture. Like new teachers, the mentored students are able to get on with the job of going to college because they acquire the skills to get through the organization and achieve a sense of control over their lives.

Growth. Through task accomplishment, there can be creative and intellectual growth. The mentee can expect to grow professionally and personally in business, school, and academic environments (Burruss, 1988; Ganser, 1992; LeCluyse, Tollefson and Borgers, 1985; Neubert and Stover, 1994). Personal growth includes the ability to develop and maintain relationships, attain a strong sense of identity and self-confidence, persist in a task, and feel ownership about one's work. Many mentees experience on-the-job growth by establishing realistic career goals and achieving a measurable increase in professional success. Particularly when offered on the job, mentoring relationships can "grow" individuals.

Having freedom to fail is a powerful growth and learning experience. Mentoring gives individuals permission to fail by allowing them to test their ideas in a safe environment. Protégés can ask their mentors questions they would be embarrassed to ask anyone else. This often protects the mentee from failing in other settings.

Growth comes for the adult with his or her awareness of being able to use decision-making skills to make choices. Collaboration with a mentor encourages the growth of these skills and the realization that shared initiative is important for personal and professional development. It can lead the adult to increased self-direction and active involvement in his or her own destiny.

The development of leadership skills is also important for personal and professional development. When student leaders were paired with mentors at the University of Minnesota (Shandley, 1989), they had higher self-perceptions of their leadership abilities than those who did not participate in the program. In the same study, mentored women had higher peer ratings on their leadership abilities than nonmentored students. In a study of school administrators, mentored principals showed changes in behaviors associated with five leadership dimensions (Ashby, 1993).

Growth on the job can be a result of mentoring relationships (LeCluyse, Tollefson, and Borgers, 1985; Murray, 1991; Ostroff and Koslowski, 1993; Shandley, 1989). New employees with mentors have an increased awareness of the organization for which they work. They can determine if the organization can support their career goals or if they should look elsewhere for opportunities. A mentored employee is less likely to be stuck in an unsuitable job or career, because his or her sponsor will not permit the waste of talent or the cost of turnover to the organization. Employees' career paths are enhanced as a result of relationships with mentors because mentors can speed up the timetable for advancement. Additionally, increased professional involvement is a result of mentoring.

Development. Separation is a natural phase in the mentoring relationship (Kram, 1983) and perhaps the most powerful for the mentee. With changes and redefinitions in the relationship come opportunities for protégés to confirm their own capabilities and autonomy. They can test their job skills and ability to work independently without the benefit of hand-holding and role modeling. Implicit in the separation is the realization that the mentor and protégé can move toward a collegial relationship. Maturity and development ultimately come from the ability to give up the previous and perhaps dependent relationship and establish a new one. When the separation is complete, both the mentor and the protégé are equipped to mentor someone new.

Benefits to Organizations

When the participants in a mentoring relationship benefit, it is not surprising that the organization would also benefit. Studies show that mentoring in a variety of settings improves recruitment efforts, hastens the induction process, improves staffing plans, increases organizational communication, increases productivity and cost effectiveness, and enhances the delivery of products and services. These are just a few of the positive outcomes of the mentoring process (Mendoza and Samuels, 1987; Murray, 1991; Selke and Wong, 1993; Terrell and Hassell, 1994).

Recruiting for positions that are unpopular or unattractive can be a problem for many organizations. Competing for employees with specialized skills can also be difficult. When mentor programs are offered as a benefit or incentive, the job opening becomes more attractive. When organizations offer mentorship programs to students, they gain an opportunity to prescreen potential new hires.

Recruiting new employees and increasing productivity is usually a costly process. This may be why mentoring programs are gaining in popularity in school settings (Ganser, 1992; Heller and Sindelar, 1991). With mentoring, beginning teachers are integrated into the school at a faster rate than their non-mentored counterparts. They are less likely to call upon their principals for answers to questions and are more likely to be inducted into the positive norms of the school. Beginning teachers have a formal way to learn the issues and practices of the school. Systematic induction also reduces turnover. When new teachers start the first day on the job in a relationship with established teachers, they are not apt to feel the sense of isolation typical of novices. Mentoring focuses on the expectation that teaching is a collaborative effort. Colleagues can be seen as source of information, particularly about technical skills and strategies. As a result, networking begins, and it has a positive impact on the new teacher's professional growth.

Training costs are reduced in a workplace that promotes mentoring. New hires can become productive more quickly. This is especially important when new personnel must fill several empty positions due to retirement of others or business growth. Mentoring sets the tone for cooperative teamwork early on; the transition from the classroom to the workplace becomes smoother and more cost efficient than before. Therefore, mentoring can be viewed as ongoing and continual staff development or inservicing.

Staffing plans in many work settings can be better implemented when new employees are mentored. Mentoring benefits the organization as an effective career development tool. Mentored employees are apt to get on a career path and stay with the company, filling various positions in the organization. Promotions can be made without leaving a vacuum in the organization. Managers can easily advance if their replacement is the person they have mentored. Succession plans can be implemented, and the developmental cycle for future leaders shortened. These benefits provide the organization with a base of technical support and power for future use, increased organizational stability, and maximized use of managerial talent and all human resources. In particular, mentoring provides meaningful work for managers with limited advancement opportunities. The wisdom of the experienced manager is therefore used advantageously.

Mentoring also reduces turnover. In an educational setting, when teachers return year after year, relationships can be nurtured so that ideas can grow and teamwork can be enhanced. New teachers can always count on their mentors, a fact that reduces any sense of isolation and frustration. Teachers learn to recognize their capabilities and are less likely to burn out and then leave the system as a solution to their problems. According to the Maslach Burnout Inventory (Mentor-Teacher Internship Program, 1992–1993, 1993), mentored teachers experience significantly less emotional exhaustion, less depersonalization, and more personal satisfaction than their nonmentored counterparts.

Mentoring also has a positive impact on the communications and general culture of the organization. Protégés enjoy the unique position of being a link between upper and lower management. They are privy to certain company information and decision-making policies and can convey this to their peers. They can facilitate the flow of communication throughout the organization. Because the nature of mentoring requires active listening and feedback, the organizational environment must foster openness and encourage the exchange of ideas. In a school setting, an esprit de corps and sense of community can develop among the faculty members, unlike the environment in which teachers remain alone and apart in their classrooms. When there is communication and an expansion of ideas, the result is increased innovation in the organization.

Institutions of higher education also benefit when faculty participate in mentoring programs (Jackson and Simpson, 1994). When mentored, women faculty have a better opportunity to succeed in gaining tenure and advancement. This enables the institution to benefit from their talents. Mentored faculty are more successful in obtaining external funding because their grant-seeking skills improve. Mentoring programs improve overall faculty effectiveness and sense of collegiality.

Productivity and cost effectiveness are vital buzzwords in any organization. Mentoring fosters a disciplined work ethic among new employees by pairing them with employees who represent the culture of the organization. Because there is a vehicle for increased communications, performance plans can be put in place with goals and measurements. An increase in goods and services can result, with an eventual impact on profitability. This is particularly felt on college campuses that are involved in programs to retain students (Mendoza and Samuels, 1987; Selke and Wong, 1993; Terrell and Hassell, 1994). When college administrators were paired with students, the program positively affected student retention as well as overall campus culture (Mendoza and Samuels, 1987). Mentored students in a community college had higher rates of return and attempted a greater number of hours, an advantage to any school as measured by student success, full-time equivalency status, and completion rates (Terrell and Hassell, 1994). Retention rates improved for minority students when they were paired in a mentoring relationship with volunteer faculty, staff, and administrators (Terrell and Hassell, 1994). Faculty and student relationships also improve.

Evidence also reveals that mentoring affects the work environment. Because mentoring is nondirective, it encourages people to reflect on their work, their personal strengths and weaknesses, and their abilities to make changes. Mentees learn how to use the resources in their organization and work within its structures. Because they have more control over their work environment, mentees can be creative and take initiative. When employees are confident about their effectiveness and abilities, they retain ownership and responsibility for decisions. Mentoring creates a climate of learning and sharing together as well as an attitude of professionalism. This relationship helps to humanize the workplace so that feelings of optimism and enthusiasm can result.

Benefits to Society

Most importantly, mentoring is a win-win situation with society at large benefiting. It maximizes the human capacity to form attachments and blends with many theories of how adults develop and change through life. Through mentoring relationships, people who might never have had the opportunity to communicate can learn from one another and gain mutual understanding and respect. Mentoring is a way to build new networks and to step beyond one's narrow roles. Talent that might have gone unnoticed has the opportunity to be expressed. Ideas that might have been lost can be productively utilized. In addition, mentoring creates a valued place for our growing number of senior citizens. And most significantly, mentoring can develop a society of self-directed and lifelong learners.

Another important feature of mentoring is that it often puts people together who would not have otherwise had any contact. The result can be an increase in understanding and appreciation, particularly when there is a focus on multigenerational and multicultural awareness and sensitivity. In a recent study of undergraduate students paired with senior citizens, the students increased their understanding about aging and developed a newfound respect and admiration for older people (Hamon and Koch, 1993). Mentors of minority students were able to understand the students' challenges and the complexity of their lives (Terrell and Hassell, 1994).

Since mentoring requires asking questions, listening, openness, and a willingness to change, it involves reaching out beyond one's familiar self and comfortable ways of doing things. A manager may spend years perfecting management skills, but when placed in a mentoring situation, he or she must draw on undiscovered talents and gain from the ability to empower rather than direct another person. Mentoring in any organization builds bridges to people, departments, and resources of which the mentor might have been unaware.

Often talents that exist in our society are underutilized; concurrently, many areas of the labor force are understaffed. Mentoring can open certain jobs previously closed to women and minorities. When female students are mentored to help them adjust to pursuing a technical career (Mentoring in 2+2 Programs, 1988), the door to typically male-dominated jobs opens. This not only changes stereotypes. It gives women access to high-paying jobs, increases the number of workers in technical fields, and raises the standard of living for women and their families. Mentoring also helps advance the timetable for women entering other professions.

Our society is aging. When seniors stay on their jobs too long, it limits the number of young people who can enter the workforce. However, some seniors are forced to leave their positions too early. The result is often a loss to their work setting and a sense of reduced significance in their lives. Mentoring provides the ideal transition for the older person who, as a mentor, can make a contribution to the workplace, to the community, and to people in need.

Individuals who function as mentors do it mostly for the intrinsic rewards. There is a pure enjoyment in working with someone who is open to learning and who values what the mentor has to say. Mentoring is positive and infectious, the reasons why many protégés eventually take on the role of mentor.

Adults are on a developmental journey. The people and events in their lives should help them reach their highest possible level. Adults do not always develop at the same rate but do progress through the same stages and transition points. Helpers in their lives assist in those transitions. Mentors as helpers in the workplace, the schools, and any place where adults face a turning point, provide the catalyst for adults to succeed.

Conclusion

The benefits of mentoring are the enhanced growth and development of both those who serve as mentors and those who are mentored. As a result, organizations where the mentoring process occurs maximize the potential of their human resources. Furthermore, the mentoring benefits are extended to the individual's life outside the work environment. Society as a whole enjoys the positive climate of people helping and empowering other people.

References

Ashby, D. "On the Job Mentoring for Administrator Renewal." *Planning and Changing,* 1993, 22 (3–4), 218–230.

Boucouvalas, M., and Krupp, J. "Adult Development and Learning." In S. B. Merriam and P. M. Cunningham (eds.), *Handbook of Adult and Continuing Education.* San Francisco: Jossey-Bass, 1989.

Bova, B. "Mentoring as a Learning Experience." In V. J. Marsick (ed.), *Learning in the Workplace.* New York: Croom Helm, 1987.

Brookfield, S. D. "Facilitating Adult Learning." In S. B. Merriam and P. M. Cunningham (eds.), *Handbook of Adult and Continuing Education.* San Francisco: Jossey-Bass, 1989.

Burruss, M. A. "Mentoring for Leadership." Paper presented at the Library Administration and Management Association President's Program, New Orleans, July 10, 1988.

Erikson, E. M. *Identity: Youth and Crisis.* New York: Norton, 1968.

Ganser, T. "The Benefits of Mentoring as Viewed by Beginning Teachers and Mentors in a State-Mandated Mentoring Program." Paper presented at the annual meeting of the Association of Teacher Educators, Orlando, Fla., Feb. 15–19, 1992.

Hamon, R. R., and Koch, D. K. "The Elder Mentor Relationship: An Experiential Learning Tool." *Educational Gerontology,* 1993, *19* (2), 147–159.

Harnish, D., and Wild, L. A. "Peer Mentoring in Higher Education: A Professional Development Strategy for Faculty." *Community College Journal of Research and Practice,* 1993, *17* (3), 271–282.

Heller, M. P., and Sindelar, N. W. *Developing an Effective Teacher Mentor Program.* Fastback no. 319. Bloomington, Ind.: Phi Delta Kappa Educational Foundation, 1991.

Jackson, W. K., and Simpson, R. D. "Mentoring New Faculty for Teaching and Research." In M. A. Wunsch (ed.), *Mentoring Revisited: Making an Impact on Individuals and Institutions.* New Directions for Teaching and Learning, no. 57. San Francisco: Jossey-Bass, 1994.

Kram, K. E. "Phases of the Mentor Relationship." *Academy of Management Journal,* 1983, *26* (4), 608–625.

LeCluyse, E. E., Tollefson, N., and Borgers, S. B. "Differences in Female Graduate Students in Relation to Mentoring." *College Student Journal,* 1985, *19,* 411–415.

Levinson, D., Darrow, C., Klein, E., Levinson, M., and McKee, B. *The Seasons of a Man's Life.* New York: Knopf, 1978.

Mendoza, J., and Samuels, C. *Faculty Mentoring System for Minority Student Retention: Year-End Report, 1986–87 Educational Year.* Glendale, Ariz.: Glendale Community College, June 3, 1987.

Mentor Teacher Internship Program, 1992–1993: OERA Report. Brooklyn, N.Y.: New York City Board of Education, 1993.

Mentoring in 2+2 Programs: LISD/ACC 2+2 Articulation Project. Waco, Tex.: Center for Occupational Research and Development, Mar. 29, 1988.

Murray, M. *Beyond the Myths and Magic of Mentoring: How to Facilitate an Effective Mentoring Program.* San Francisco: Jossey-Bass, 1991.

Neubert, G., and Stover, L. T. *Peer Coaching in Teacher Education.* Fastback no. 371. Bloomington, Ind.: Phi Delta Kappa Educational Foundation, 1994.

Ostroff, C., and Koslowski, S. W. "The Role of Mentoring in the Information Gathering Processes of Newcomers During Early Organizational Socialization." *Journal of Vocational Behavior,* 1993, *42* (2), 170–183.

Selke, M. J., and Wong, T. D. "The Mentoring-Empowered Model: Facilitating Communication in Graduate Advisement." Paper presented at the conference of the National Academic Advising Association, Bloomington, Minn., Apr. 23, 1993.

Shandley, T. C. "The Use of Mentors for Leadership Development." *NASPA Journal,* 1989, *27* (1), 60–66.

Terrell, M. C., and Hassell, R. K. "Mentoring Undergraduate Minority Students: An Overview, Survey, and Model Program." In M. A. Wunsch (ed.), *Mentoring Revisited: Making an Impact on Individuals and Institutions.* New Directions for Teaching and Learning, no. 57. San Francisco: Jossey-Bass, 1994.

Susan F. Schulz is a proprietary school consultant for private vocational schools and is working on a doctoral degree in educational leadership at Florida Atlantic University.

Is mentoring today a vehicle for assimilation or pluralism? Institutions and individuals must explore their cultural assumptions and develop specific strategies for mentoring in a multicultural society.

Mentoring to Diversity: A Multicultural Approach

Yvonne Enid Gonzalez Rodriguez

Institutionally sponsored mentoring programs are one vehicle for enhancing personal and professional growth. However, organizations and the individuals who sponsor and implement mentoring programs must be aware that mentoring in a diverse society may become another mechanism for the control of traditionally marginalized or excluded groups. Mentoring initiatives may become vehicles for skirting the larger issues of discrimination based on racism, sexism, ageism, classism, xenophobia, heterosexism, and ableism. Existing models of counseling and pedagogy as well as theories of development have been conceived from a Euro-American, upper-middle-class, and male perspective. These models perpetuate a monocultural perspective and a scaffold for the reproduction of the status quo. Mentoring in a diverse society is ambitious and demanding. It requires knowledge, skills, openness, fairness, discipline, commitment, and courage. Institutional value systems, goals, academic content, and procedures, and the outcomes of all that is supported by the institution, will be called into question. The institution, the philosophical stance of the academic discipline, the mentors, and the protégés will need to be examined, challenged, and critiqued.

The purpose of this chapter is to explore issues of diversity related to mentoring in a multicultural society such as the United States of America. The intention is to raise questions regarding the intent and outcomes of mentoring culturally diverse individuals who find themselves in predominantly white settings. Another objective is to examine the applicability of existing models and to propose strategies for mentoring to diversity.

NEW DIRECTIONS FOR ADULT AND CONTINUING EDUCATION, no. 66, Summer 1995 © Jossey-Bass Inc., Publishers

Issues in Multicultural Mentoring

A discussion of the major issues in multicultural mentoring needs to begin with a definition of terms. First, we can define *multiculturalism* "as a broad-based construct that not only is relevant to all cultural groups [by gender, race, class, ethnicity, age, religion, sexual orientation, and physical ability] but also respects the complexity of all people based on their personal dimensions of identity" (Arrendondo, Psalti, and Cella, 1993, p. 2). Second, we can define *multicultural mentoring* as the mentoring of individuals from diverse cultural backgrounds, from traditionally underrepresented populations, and of many cognitive perspectives.

Bearing those definitions in mind, we can now examine some of the major issues. Also keeping in mind that multicultural mentoring is a process, we must have a developmental perspective. No one has the "right" way or "best" practice. There are no scripts and never can be, as the process responds to the diversity of its clients. Multicultural mentoring is critical pedagogy. It should be similar to Giroux's radical education (1992), which requires the questioning of the institution and its mission as well as the questioning of the cultural assumptions of the disciplines. It also requires a public mission of social equity and democratic inclusion. Multicultural mentoring creates spaces for differences and celebrates democracy by facilitating inclusion and participation. It allows learning to take place while guarding that no one's voice is silenced. Multicultural mentoring reminds the institution and the mentors that "the referent out of which we operate is white, upper-middle-class logic that not only modulizes but actually silences subordinate voices" (Giroux, 1992, p. 14). I would add that the referent is also male logic.

There is a widespread belief that where mentoring programs exist, they become a critical component of effectiveness in accomplishing the goals of the organization as well as the goals of the persons involved. The perspective that mentoring is highly beneficial has been documented in business, undergraduate, and graduate education (Jacobi, 1991). It is also evident from the numerous mentoring programs initiated since the mid seventies.

The majority of the literature on mentoring comes from three fields: education, management, and psychology. The impact on personal relations (particularly between mentor and protégé) and on educational and professional experience as well as on outcomes continues to be the focus of much research. Some issues of concern are the variety of mentoring programs, their lack of commonality of purpose, their duration, and their formality. Glaring in the literature is the lack of an operational definition of mentoring. In effect, this vagueness as to what the concept of mentoring is and what it is not, complicates further the notion of multicultural mentoring and our ability to address issues of diversity through mentoring.

Surface issues in multicultural mentoring include the importance of gender, racial, ethnic, or class similarity between the mentor and the protégé and of the physical and social environment in which the mentoring takes place.

Issues such as the matching of values and goals—for example, worldviews and personal and professional goals—are at a second, deeper level of concern. Of central concern, are the issues of the operational theories of the institution and the operational theories of the mentor and the protégé on the subject of diversity and multiculturalism.

Matching Cultural Characteristics. In a review of the literature on mentoring and undergraduate academic success, Jacobi (1991) found the researchers to be divided in their support for the importance of a match in gender, race, ethnicity, and so forth between mentor and protégé in mentoring programs. There is evidence of both cross-gender and cross-race pairs having difficulty in establishing and maintaining the mentoring relationship. These problems are reported to range from mild to severe. For example, in studies where women mentored other women, the women protégés reported having more mentors and experiencing positive effects from mentoring. In studies where there were few same gender mentors for women, women reported difficulty in identifying and establishing mentoring relationships. An interesting note, however, is that male researchers concluded that a match in cultural characteristics made no difference while female researchers concluded that it did make a difference. The gender of the researcher may have been a factor in the conclusions drawn from the analysis in each case. However, a word of caution is needed. There have been few studies that have had similarity of multicultural characteristics between mentor and protégé as a focus of research, and those that exist crossed disciplines and professions, used different methodologies, and are more than ten years old. Therefore, data from the studies cannot be compared. No study, to my knowledge, has used class as a variable in the mentoring match.

In fields where women, people of color, and people with disabilities may be an underrepresented group, the matching of cultural characteristics may not be an issue. In a review of the mentoring literature in management, Noe (1988) suggests that women are less likely than men to have mentors, while Burke (1984) found no gender difference among managers participating in his research. But these studies suffer from the same methodological problems as those mentioned earlier. There needs to be focused research on the cultural similarities between the mentor and protégé and their impact on the mentoring relation and its efficacy.

In the review of the literature on mentoring that suggested that mentors and protégés experience from severe difficulty to no difficulty in establishing and maintaining mentoring relationships based on pairing for gender and/or race, Jacobi (1991) also found that while much of the descriptive and theoretical literature about higher education mentoring for students of color reports cross-race and cross-gender initiatives to be effective (Moses, 1989; Pounds, 1987; Rowe, 1989), in practice many programs strive to pair students with mentors of their own gender, racial, or ethnic backgrounds (Meznek, McGrath, and Garcia, 1989; Oestereichen, 1987; Johnson, 1989). For example, in mentoring programs where the goals are to retain specific groups of people—for example, to retain African American males in college—program administrators have made conscious efforts to pair for cultural characteristics. Overall, although the literature on cross-gender and cross-race mentoring pairs is inconclusive as to the advantages and disadvantages of matching for cultural characteristics, the reality is there are not enough women and people of color in established positions in some organizations to serve as mentors.

Free Choice Mentoring. Another surface issue for multicultural mentoring is the availability of free choice mentoring versus formal mentoring programs for women, people of color, and people with disabilities. In her review of the research on mentoring, Jacobi (1991) stated mixed findings on the efficacy of formal mentoring, that is, where mentors are assigned to students or employees, in contrast to mentoring relationships that develop naturally as a result of mutual interest or personal relationships. However, cultural traditions such as old boys networks and historically exclusionary practices within some organizations toward women, people of color, and people of diverse cultural backgrounds in higher education and in managerial positions have made it increasingly difficult for women and people of color to find such naturally developing relationships and true mentors. A true, or genuine, mentor is behaviorally competent in and psychologically committed to a mentoring relationship. Johnson (1989) and Blackwell (1989) both report that true mentoring for women and people of color is rare, especially at the undergraduate level.

Institutional Climate. The institutional climate is another variable in the physical and social environment of institutions that influences multicultural mentoring. Many institutions and organizations pay little attention to diversity, especially as it relates to women, people of color, and people with various other cultural characteristics. For the majority of educators, managers, and decision makers, multiculturalism in any form is viewed as the domain—that is, the field of action, knowledge, or influence—of ethnic and racial minority people. It is viewed as ultimately owned only by minorities. Therefore, just as multicultural mentoring requires the mentor to develop multiple cultural perspectives, the sponsoring agencies must develop into multicultural institutions. Bensiman and Tierney (1992–1993, p. 4) urge the development of a comprehensive policy regarding the shaping of a multicultural campus in higher education that "will sustain ongoing change in the culture of the organization."This campus will also set a tone, a mission, and a vision that is multicultural. Organizations involved in mentoring to diversity need to evaluate their structures, norms, and values to identify their current understanding of differences, because "a monocultural perspective represents a fundamentally different framework for understanding differences than does a multicultural one" (Nieto, 1992, p. 276).

Impact of Values and Goals. The institutional climate is an important surface issue of mentoring programs. However, the climate issue spans into the second level of issues, that is, values and goals. "Every organization has an avowed mission, a set of goals and expressed values about its function" (Putnam and Burke, 1992, p. 64). The individuals involved in the mentoring program, if they are striving toward multicultural mentoring, must have an understanding of their organization's mission and culture. The values embedded in the processes and the goals of the organization must support the complexity of mentoring to diversity with multiple cultural perspectives. The challenge in acquiring a cultural understanding of an organization lies in the multifaceted nature of any organization. The values expressed by the organization's members may or may not be current, supported, and/or verifiable by examining the evidence available to the general public.

The values and goals inherent in the "epistemological premises on which the classical model of mentoring is based preclude the kind of mutual revisioning, teaching, and learning required for integrating gender, race, and class into the curriculum, process, and climate of higher education" (Okorodudu, 1995, p. 3). The traditional model of mentoring imposes a monocultural perspective and an assimilationist goal. Built into the traditional model is a power relationship. The mentor is older and wiser; therefore, he or she holds all the power. It is assumed that the protégé will continue the work of the mentor and uphold the status quo. The mentoring relationship is not collaborative or communal but rather hierarchical. This traditional model is the antithesis of multicultural mentoring as described in this chapter.

Operational Theories. The third level of issues deals with the operational theories of the organization and the members involved in the mentoring program. The "operational theories of any organization are the basic assumptions its members hold about the meaning of what they do in their group" (Putnam and Burke, 1992, p. 65). These theories tend to be invisible in the organization and taken for granted by the participating members. Operational theories may include views on human nature, such as the belief that people are basically good, kind, and persevering, or not. They may include beliefs about culture, time, respect, ethics, and even knowledge. The operational theories held by organizations and their members are each group's cultural underpinnings. Therefore, they may not be within the immediate awareness of the group members, and the people who function by them are often not conscious of them (Putnam and Burke, 1992). This makes them difficult to identify and examine. People may not have examined the theories that drive their behaviors in a very long time. And, I believe, when we do critically examine these theories, it will become evident that gender, race, ethnicity, class, sexual orientation, and variance in ability played little or no role in their development.

A very important operational theory in mentoring to diversity or multicultural mentoring is Minnich's theory of "alterity," that is, one's view of the other (1990). Minnich explains alterity as one person's view of another person as strange, different, inferior or deficient, and distant from himself or herself. An example of this phenomenon was Columbus's view of the indigenous peoples of the Americas as estranged others, which led him to justify inhumane treatment and deceitfulness. The concept of alterity allowed Columbus to view these people as subhuman when he compared their ways to the values, beliefs, and practices of the Europeans. When a person takes this posture, his or her operational theory is that humans of a particular kind (gender, race, age, class, ethnicity, religion, sexual orientation, and so forth) are the only ones who are significant and worthy and thus they are the ones who should set the standards for all people. Minnich presents alterity as one of four root problems in philosophy. She explains that this operational theory is faulty logic because it universalizes to the particular. Minnich states, "It is very strange to maintain that one small group of people is simultaneously the essence, the inclusive term, the norm, and the ideal for all" (p. 39). Yet it is exactly this kind of unconscious thinking that promotes a monocultural perspective and assimilationist goals in the mentoring program.

Another important operational theory in any institution will concern race. What are the racial assumptions of the institution, its members, the mentor program, and in particular, the mentors? Has there been internalization of the negative societal beliefs surrounding people of color in this country? Is racism denied? Are people of color looked at from a deficit perspective? For example, are there lower performance expectations for people of color? Are they assigned less rigorous and challenging tasks? These beliefs would be detrimental to multicultural mentoring, the organization, and the person holding the beliefs.

Existing Mentoring Models

A review of the literature in the fields of education, management, and psychology reveals a growing increase in attention to mentoring programs. Over the last ten years alone, there have been hundreds of such programs implemented. The literature suggests that these have little in common, other than a goal to assist in the success of the protégé. Merriam (1983, p. 169) has proposed that "the phenomenon of mentoring is not clearly conceptualized. . . . Mentoring appears to mean one thing to developmental psychologists, another thing to business people, and a third thing to those in academic settings." Jacobi (1991) found a similar variety. The result is that although the literature reports particular programs addressing an organization's or group's unique needs, specific models have not been identified and tested in various settings and then proven to be applicable to multicultural mentoring. Even though multicultural mentoring requires a developmental perspective that embodies an ongoing process and excludes using one model as a definitive model, I did expect to be able to classify models for possible inclusion in this chapter. But the reality is that few programs address multiculturalism. Many programs have targeted minority group members as protégés. However, these programs have not altered the cultural structure of the organization to accommodate cultural differences. Instead, most programs have an assimilationist goal for the protégé, are politically expedient for the institution, and have a tendency to perpetuate the status quo as well as the privileged position of the group(s) in power.

Strategies for Mentoring to Diversity

Given the situation I have described, what can we do to implement mentoring to diversity in our organizations? We can start at the very beginning and take nothing for granted. We can define what our organizations mean by mentoring and hold conversations on the concept of multiculturalism. If either of these constructs, mentoring or multiculturalism, remains vague or lacks clarity and specificity, we run the risk that the program will be trivialized, marginalized, or accused of perpetuating monocultural values and norms. The people directly involved with the mentoring program should assess the degree to which other institutional actors support the program. Once these initial tasks have been accomplished, we can select a theoretical base that emphasizes the contextual nature of learning. Multicultural mentoring recognizes that learning is an active process that is deeply contextualized and also that learning is developmental.

The physical and social environment of our organizations need to be assessed in light of mentoring to diversity. This environment includes the people, mission, structure, and curriculum. People within the organization should be representative of the diversity that exists in the larger society. Since it is the people who create the organization's culture, the mission of the organization must speak to social equity, respect for differences, and democratic inclusion. Anything less would perpetuate a monocultural model, regardless of the demographic composition of the workforce or student body.

The structure of our organizations as well as the structure of our mentoring programs must reflect a multicultural orientation. In order to assess the organizational structure, difficult questions need to be asked and answered honestly. What is the degree of cultural representation among the decision makers? Who promotes diversity within the organizational structure, and how is it promoted? Despite much debate surrounding multicultural curricular projects, most curricula still project a monocultural, Eurocentric bias. Our organizations need to identify where there is bias in the curriculum and to make it explicit while working to transform it. Faculty in all disciplines need to develop pedagogical strategies for multicultural teaching.

Strategies for Mentors

New directions are needed for training multiculturally skilled mentors. Demographic projections for some states (for example, California) predict that by the year 2000, there will be no group in the majority and that African Americans; Latinos, as a cohort group; and Asians will outnumber today's majority white population. Our organizations will have to develop plans to address the challenge of training mentors for mentoring to diversity. Most mentors were educated in monocultural environments, which to some extent have worked for them. As a result, mentors need to become multicultural people before they can address mentoring to diversity. This will require transformational changes. Nieto (1992) presents a three-step process: first, simply learn more (read, attend multicultural events and pluralistic activities); second, confront your own racism and bias (as the product of a society that is racist and stratified by gender, class, and language, every person has internalized some of that society's messages); and third, learn to see reality from a variety of perspectives.

For most mentors this requires a dramatic shift in their worldview. It means learning new things and unlearning old ones.

Conclusion

Institutional values, goals, and operational theories need to be examined in the light of mentoring to diversity. Many values held and assumptions made within a Western, male, upper-middle-class construct may not be applicable and, instead of promoting multiple perspectives, may lead to mentoring that aims for homogenization or conformity to one viewpoint. For mentoring to be a change agent for the institution as well as the person being mentored, the assumptions underlying traditional models of hierarchical mentoring must be challenged to allow for democratic participation in the institution as well as in the society at large. A vision of mentoring that emphasizes the acceptance of difference as enriching the worldview and contributions of an institution could transform mentoring practices, making them congruent with our diverse society.

References

Arrendondo, P., Psalti, A., and Cella, K. "The Woman Factor in Multicultural Counseling." *Counseling and Human Development,* 1993, *25* (8), 1–8.

Bensiman, S. M., and Tierney, W. G. "Shaping the Multicultural Campus: Strategies for Administrators." *College Board Review,* Late Winter 1992–1993, no. 166.

Blackwell, J. E. "Mentoring: An Action Strategy for Increasing Minority Faculty." *Academe,* 1989, *75,* 8–14.

Burke, R. J. "Mentors in Organizations." *Group and Organizational Studies,* 1984, *9,* 353–372.

Giroux, H. *Border Crossings.* New York: Routledge & Kegan Paul, 1992.

Jacobi, M. "Mentoring and Undergraduate Academic Success: A Literature Review." *Review of Educational Research,* 1991, *61* (4), 505–532.

Johnson, C. S. "Mentoring Programs." In M. L. Upcraft, J. N. Gardner, and Associates, *The Freshman Year Experience: Helping Students Survive and Succeed in College.* San Francisco: Jossey-Bass, 1989.

Merriam, S. B. "Mentors and Protégés: A Critical Review of the Literature." *Adult Education Quarterly,* 1983, *33* (3), 161–173.

Meznek, J., McGrath, P., and Garcia, F. *The Puente Project: A Report of the Board of Governors, California Community Colleges.* Sacramento: Office of the Chancellor, California Community Colleges, 1989. (ED 307 920)

Minnich, E. *Transforming Knowledge.* Philadelphia: Temple University Press, 1990.

Moses, Y. T. *Black Women in Academe: Issues and Strategies.* Washington, D.C.: Association of American Colleges, 1989. (ED 311 817)

Nieto, S. *Affirming Diversity: The Socio-Political Context of Multicultural Education.* White Plains, N.Y.: Longman, 1992.

Noe, R. A. "Women and Mentoring: A Review and Research Agenda." *Academy of Management Review,* 1988, *13,* 65–78.

Oestereichen, M. "Effectiveness of Peer Tutors/Mentors for Disadvantaged Students at Brooklyn College: Preliminary Analysis." *Linkages,* 1987, *5,* 27–33. (ED 296 021)

Okorodudu, C. "Collaborative Mentoring: Transforming the Nature of Academic Work." Paper presented at the Multicultural Workshop at Rowan College of New Jersey, Mar. 8, 1995.

Pounds, A. W. "Black Students' Needs on Predominantly White Campuses." In D. J. Wright (ed.), *Responding to the Needs of Today's Minority Students*. New Directions for Student Services, no. 38. San Francisco: Jossey-Bass, 1987.

Putnam, J., and Burke, B.. *Organizing and Managing Classroom Learning Communities*. New York: McGraw-Hill, 1992.

Rowe, M. P. "What Actually Works? The One-to-One Approach." In C. S. Pearson, D. L. Sharlick, and J. B. Touchton (eds.), *Educating the Majority: Women Challenge Education in Higher Education*. New York: American Council on Education/Macmillan, 1989.

YVONNE ENID GONZALEZ RODRIGUEZ is assistant professor of education at Rowan College of New Jersey.

Effective, productive mentoring alliances are the culmination of a complex developmental process. Knowing the resources that can build a basic framework for this process is important for mentors, mentees, and organizations.

Strategies and Resources for Enhancing Mentoring Relationships

Linda Marie Golian

Mentoring is an important component in human development and is a significant adult education training and developmental tool for personal life enrichment and professional growth (Hunt and Michael, 1983; Levinson and others, 1978; Sheehy, 1976). Fostering effective mentoring relationships in adult learning environments is a complex process demanding flexibility and an understanding of human interrelations. It requires commitment from the organization, mentors, and mentees. Whether you are just beginning a mentoring relationship or are revamping an effective program within an organization, a substantial reliance upon personnel, practical program advice, and reference resources is essential.

The purpose of this chapter is to present strategies and resources for individuals interested in mentoring. The first half highlights several practical professional development strategies that can strengthen mentoring relationships. The latter half features an annotated bibliography offering insights into the various applications and critical issues of effective mentoring relationships.

Professional Development Strategies

Mentoring is just one of many developmental strategies available for adults seeking personal or career growth. This section presents several successful strategies used in a wide variety of adult learning environments to foster career enrichment. It includes the use of professional association activities, mentoring association activities, networking activities, and electronic communications.

Professional Associations. Serving a crucial role in the development of their members, professional associations act as natural clearing houses for effective mentoring relationships and programs (Darkenwald and Merriam, 1982). These organizations provide a vision for their members while simultaneously serving as a valuable resource of professional development opportunities for those who practice, and those who wish to practice, in the field (Brockett, 1989).

Many professional associations exist on multiple levels, including local, state, regional, national, and international affiliations. They logically support the fundamental mission of the profession, with the national or international affiliation acting as an unifying umbrella for various segments and interest groups (Brockett, 1991). The organizational hierarchy of many associations with local and regional ties supports a form of progressive mentoring for aspiring adult members as they pass through the gradual maze of local to national professional involvement.

One mentoring endeavor supported by most professional associations is the active recruitment of new members. Another mentoring venture is the continual grooming of new leaders who will continue to provide the profession and the organization with vision, networks, resources, energy, and challenges.

Mentoring Associations. In addition to the mentoring services provided by specific professional associations, several organizations devoted to the field of mentoring are worth noting.

International Mentoring Association, Office of Conferences and Institutes, Western Michigan University, Kalamazoo, MI 49008–5161.

Established in 1989, the International Mentoring Association coordinates a public forum for supporting and enhancing effective mentoring strategies and offers various membership categories for students, individuals, and institutions. The association sponsors an annual conference, with published proceedings available for purchase. Membership includes the quarterly newsletter *Mentoring Connection* and access to *CONSLT-L,* an electronic network focusing on mentoring issues.

The Mentoring Institute, Inc., ICM International Centre for Mentoring, 675 Inglewood Avenue, West Vancouver, B.C., Canada V7T 1X4.

Established in 1978, The Mentoring Institute (TMI) provides consultation, design, training, and evaluation for mentoring programs. Products available from the association include traditional print materials and videotapes. Membership includes the quarterly journal *Mentoring International* (previously known as the *International Journal of Mentoring,* February 1987 through Autumn 1988), and *Mentor Ink Newsletter.*

National Association of Tutoring (formerly known as the National Organization of Tutoring and Mentoring Centers), Jacksonville State University, Ramona Wood Building, Room 105, 700 Pelham Road North, Jacksonville, AL 36265–9982.

Established in 1991, the National Association of Tutoring supports a program of training college students to tutor and mentor elementary and secondary school children. The association provides information and conducts research in the areas of intergenerational mentoring, tutoring, and leadership techniques.

Networking. Additional developmental activities sponsored by professional associations include continuing education workshops, seminars, and conferences. These learning smorgasbords help professionals increase their knowledge concerning innovations, research, changing priorities, and opportunities within their fields. As a bonus, conferences with exhibits allow professionals to view and sample new products and services firsthand.

Conferences and other continuing education forums provide an ideal environment for fostering networking relationships because of the opportunities for face-to-face meetings and work with others who share common interests and concerns. At these forums, beginning and senior-level professionals have the chance to share ideas that traditional workplace barriers might prevent. Individuals who regularly attend these learning opportunities quickly build a network of professional resource colleagues who are only a telephone call or electronic message away.

Electronic Communications. Advances in electronic communications support and enhance networking activities. This resource is often used to co-author a research article, share professional association news, or answer basic questions posed by a neophyte member.

Today's technological advances allow worldwide communication for individuals with access to a computer and a modem. Electronic mail is a medium that increases opportunities for networking with others in a timely and cost-efficient manner compared with traditional mail or telephone services (Brockett, 1991). Individuals posting questions to electronic bulletin boards receive rapid feedback, with responses covering a wide variety of perspectives.

Perhaps most important is this resource's ability to break down networking barriers. Electronic networking allows individuals of varying professional rank to communicate as equals and breaks down time and distance barriers for colleagues communicating from various time zones.

Mentoring Resources

Professional research and reading is another successful avenue of career enrichment. Successful implementation of mentoring as a developmental strategy requires an understanding of the complexities, possibilities, shortcomings, roles, and functions of this tool (Bey and Holmes, 1992).

A brief literature review reveals numerous mentoring resources in a wide variety of disciplines. It is crucial, however, to realize that effective mentoring follows universal principles, whether the program is instituted in a vocational school, community college, church, or corporation. The basic criteria for good and effective mentoring remain the same, regardless of the discipline or profession.

Recently a tremendous growth in the application of mentoring programs has led to an increase in research publications. It is beyond the scope of this chapter to provide a comprehensive bibliography of these resources. Therefore, I have annotated materials that will be useful in a variety of learning environments. These materials include bibliographies, books, book chapters and miscellaneous documents, journal articles, and workbooks.

Bibliographies

Gray, M. M. (ed.). *Mentoring and Coaching: An Annotated Bibliography.* West Vancouver, B.C.: The Mentoring Institute, 1989.

A companion to the Gray and Gray 1986 bibliography below, this work covers the period from 1986 to late 1989, with approximately 550 new entries, highlighting dissertations, conference papers, videotapes, films, books, and journal articles.

Gray, W. A., and Gray, M. M. (eds.). *Mentoring: A Comprehensive Annotated Bibliography of Important References.* Vancouver, B.C.: International Association for Mentoring, 1986.

This resource contains approximately 800 entries of materials published prior to 1986. Entries, listed in one of seven categories, include dissertations, conference papers, films, books, and journal articles. Abstracts are approximately 40 to 150 words in length.

Noller, R. B., and Frey, B. R. *Mentoring: An Annotated Bibliography.* Buffalo, N.Y.: Bearly Limited, 1983.

A comprehensive survey of literature from 1962 to 1983 that includes books, journal articles, and dissertation citations, all arranged alphabetically by authors' last names. A matrix guide is designed to help readers locate items relating to seventeen mentoring focus areas.

Books

Bey, T. M., and Holmes, C. T. *Mentoring: Contemporary Principles and Issues.* Reston, Va.: Association of Teacher Educators, 1992.

Written to support the Association of Teacher Educators' goal of developing the human potential of all educational professionals, this book focuses upon useful principles in developing adult mentoring for network building and team leadership.

Caldwell, B., and Carter, E. (eds.). *The Return of the Mentor: Strategies for Workplace Learning.* Washington, D.C.: Falmer Press, 1993.

Caldwell and Carter supply specific suggestions for applying mentoring strategies to transform the workplace of the 1990s. Subdivided into three different working environments—education, health, and industry—the book furnishes specific program examples for these professional areas.

Clutteruck, D. *Everyone Needs a Mentor: How to Foster Talent Within the Organization.* Wimbledon, England: Institute of Personnel Management, 1985.

This book expands the concept of mentoring as an alternative method of career development and emphasizes how mentoring benefits the mentor, mentee, and the organization. Five mentoring case studies are included.

Cohen, N. H. *Mentoring Adult Learners: A Guide for Educators and Trainers.* Malabar, Fla.: Krieger, 1995.

Cohen approaches mentoring as an adult development process of learning and presents information from the fields of adult psychology and applied interpersonal communications. He offers real-life examples, based upon adult mentoring theory research, and provides validated self-assessment instruments for mentors to measure their effectiveness.

Collins, N. W. *Professional Women and Their Mentors: A Practical Guide to Mentoring for the Woman Who Wants to Get Ahead.* Englewood Cliffs, N.J.: Prentice Hall, 1983.

Specifically written for women with strong desires to actively seek out professional development activities and mentoring opportunities, this work addresses many gender-specific questions posed by both women and men involved in mentoring relationships.

Daloz, L. A. *Effective Teaching and Mentoring: Realizing the Transformational Power of Adult Learning Experiences.* San Francisco: Jossey-Bass, 1986.

Based upon adult development theories, this book demonstrates how mentors can provide mentees with the blend of challenge, support, and inspiration necessary for personal, intellectual and professional growth. It includes real-life accounts of mentoring relationships.

Evans, T. W. *Mentors: Making a Difference in Our Public Schools.* Princeton, N.J.: Peterson's Guides, 1992.

Designed to help school systems attract community leaders for various school mentoring programs, *Mentors* provides examples of ways nonteaching adults can assist with both student intergenerational and teacher mentoring programs for the benefit of the entire community.

Kram, K. E. *Mentoring at Work: Developmental Relationships in Organizational Life.* Glenview, Ill.: Scott, Foresman, 1985.

Kram explains how mentoring relationships in organizations can enhance an individual's professional development in early, middle, and later career years. She also includes background information on the various phases and stages of mentoring and additional professional development strategies.

Maack, M. N., and Passet, J. *Aspirations and Mentoring in an Academic Environment.* Westport, Conn.: Greenwood, 1994.

This work examines career development opportunities and obstacles for female library science professors. Through a cross-generational study, it highlights how mentoring has affected the lives of many female academic professionals, and it reflects on the important changes in women's status and opportunities over the past five decades.

Murray, M. *Beyond the Myths and Magic of Mentoring: How to Facilitate an Effective Mentoring Program.* San Francisco: Jossey-Bass, 1991.

Murray provides step-by-step guidelines for a establishing a cost-effective mentoring program that fosters employee professional development. She explains how effective mentoring is a personally rewarding experience for mentors and contributes to optimal organizational performance.

Phillips-Jones, L. *Mentors and Proteges.* New York: Arbor House, 1982.

Helpful for both the mentor and the mentee, this book explains how effective mentoring is a complex process that requires effort from both parties. Case studies and anecdotes drawn from interviews conducted with participants in actual mentoring programs are included.

Shea, F. G. *Mentoring: Helping Employees Reach Their Full Potential.* New York: American Management Association, 1994.

This concise eighty-nine-page booklet addresses effective behaviors for mentors and the responsibilities of mentees. It also comments on the current renewed interest in mentoring in corporate America.

Sullivan, C. G. *How to Mentor in the Midst of Change.* Alexandria, Va.: Association for Supervision and Curriculum Development, 1992.

Sullivan provides suggestions and background information for individuals interested in becoming mentors, discusses concepts and activities associated with mentoring, and concludes with suggestions on how to develop a customized mentoring plan.

Wunsch, M. A. (ed.). *Mentoring Revisited: Making an Impact on Individuals and Institutions.* New Directions for Teaching and Learning, no. 57. San Francisco: Jossey-Bass, 1994.

This monograph places mentoring in an academic learning context. The various chapters highlight strategies that use mentoring programs for professional development, tenure passage, promotion, academic advancement, and retirement preparation.

Zey, M. G. *The Mentor Connection.* Homewood, Ill.: Business One Irwin, 1984.

Zey focuses upon the ways connecting with a mentor can affect mentees' careers, increase their chances of success, and enhance their quality of life. This book provides excellent background information on the roles, functions, phases, and characteristics of mentoring programs.

Book Chapters and Miscellaneous Documents

Bova, B. "Mentoring as a Learning Experience." In V. J. Marsick (ed.), *Learning in the Workplace.* New York: Croom Helm, 1987.

Based upon the author's research, this chapter concludes that mentoring relationships are vital to the career development of newcomers in any profession. It also provides numerous suggestions for potential mentees looking for mentors and advice for mentors desiring to foster relationships of mutual respect and trust.

Daloz, L. A. "Mentorship." In M. W. Galbraith (ed.), *Adult Learning Methods.* Malabar, Fla.: Krieger, 1990.

Daloz provides a brief history of mentoring in higher education and discusses his research in creating a definition of mentoring. He includes information on the roles and functions of mentors, addresses many limitations and problems of mentoring, and provides suggestions and possible evaluation procedures.

Daresh, J. C., and Playko, M. A. *A Method for Matching Leadership Mentors and Protégés.* Paper presented at the annual meeting of the Association for Supervision and Curriculum Development, New Orleans, Apr. 1992. (ED 344 315)

This paper describes a study that used an adaptation of the Sayers-Kirsch Leadership Matrix to match mentors with beginning teachers based upon personality types. It describes four mentor-protégé styles: supportive, directive, facilitative, and scientific.

Galbraith, M. W., and Zelenak, B. S. "Adult Learning Methods and Techniques." In M. W. Galbraith (ed.), *Facilitating Adult Learning: A Transactional Process.* Malabar, Fla.: Krieger, 1991.

Galbraith and Zelenak summarize seven transactional methods and techniques useful for enhancing educational encounters between adults. The mentoring technique portion comments on the lack of an agreed-upon definition of mentoring and describes mentor and mentee roles. The chapter concludes with the highlights of several functions of effective mentoring.

Griffin, E. V., and Ervin, N. R. *Innovative Practices and Developments in Student Mentoring.* Charleston: Division of Student Affairs, West Virginia State College, 1990. (ED 323 893)

This training manual for establishing a college mentoring program for newly enrolled students, with a special emphasis upon minority and first-generation students, describes a program concerned with both the cognitive and affective development of student mentees.

Otto, M. L. "Mentoring: An Adult Developmental Perspective." In M. A. Wunsch (ed.), *Mentoring Revisited: Making an Impact on Individuals and Institutions*. New Directions for Teaching and Learning, no. 57. San Francisco: Jossey-Bass, 1994.

Otto focuses on the changing needs of adult mentors and mentees as they mature chronologically and professionally through the various phases of a mentoring program. The chapter emphasizes the different developmental tasks and kinds of mentoring support associated with beginning and later career stages.

Journal Articles

Bolton, E. B. "A Conceptual Analysis of the Mentor Relationship in the Career Development of Women." *Adult Education*, 1980, *30* (4), 195–207.

This conceptual analysis of the mentor relationship as an aspect of social learning and professional development for women is divided into three sections that discuss the socializing and modeling process, mentor relationships as functions of social learning, and the lack of mentoring relationships for women.

Harnish, D., and Wild, L. A. "Peer Mentoring in Higher Education: A Professional Development Strategy for Faculty." *Community College Journal of Research and Practice,* 1993, *17* (3), 271–282.

This article emphasizes the growing recognition of peer mentoring as a learning strategy and highlights four peer mentoring projects developed under a federal Title II grant for professional development and instructional improvement.

Healy, C. C., and Welchert, A. J. "Mentoring Relationships: A Definition to Advance Research and Practice." *Educational Researcher,* 1990, *19* (9), 17–21.

Healy and Welchert provide a definition of mentoring grounded in contextual development theory, a review of literature, and the findings of past investigations.

Hunt, D. M., and Michael, C. "Mentorship: A Career Training and Development Tool." *Academy of Management Review,* 1983, *8,* 475–485.

This article suggests a framework for the study of mentorship that includes organizational climate, mentor characteristics, mentee characteristics, and stages of relationships. Possible program outcomes for mentors, mentees, and organizations are described, and research issues and possible areas for future mentoring research are summarized.

Jacobi, M. "Mentoring and Undergraduate Academic Success: A Literature Review." *Review of Educational Research,* 1991, *61* (4), 505–532.

This significant and organized review of literature on mentorship and learning environments addresses the major concern of the lack of an operational definition of mentoring and summarizes various definitions from the fields of education, management, and psychology. Jacobi concludes by investigating the question, "Is there a link between academic success and participation in mentoring programs?"

Merriam, S. B. "Mentors and Protégés: A Critical Review of the Literature." *Adult Education Quarterly,* Spring 1983, *33* (3), 161–173.

This review of the literature was written to evaluate how the use of mentoring has been substantiated by research. Information is categorized under three sections: the mentoring phenomenon in adult growth and development, mentoring in the business world, and mentoring in academic settings.

Workbooks

Berry, D., Cadwell, C., and Fehrmann, J. *50 Activities for Coaching/Mentoring.* Amherst, Mass.: HRD Press, 1993.

This workbook contains a wide variety of activities from the simple and lighthearted to the complex and risky. The mix reflects the authors' belief that different approaches are required to reach different people at different levels. Each activity includes a statement on objectives, discussions of how to conduct the activity and how to review the participants' experiences, and a description of learning points to discuss.

Newton, A., Bergstrom, K., Brennan, N., Dunne, K., Gilbert, C., Ibarguen, N., Perez-Selles, M., and Thomas, E. *Mentoring: A Resource and Training Guide for Educators.* Andover, Mass.: Research Laboratory of Educational Improvement of the Northeast and Islands, 1994.

Developed to help both new and experienced educators become reflective practitioners through integrating mentoring programs into the learning environment, this workbook suggests an abundance of activities for fostering effective peer mentoring programs.

Ropp, S. *One on One: Making the Most of Your Mentoring Relationship.* Newton, Kans.: Faith and Life Press, 1993.

Written from a Christian youth ministry perspective, this source includes an extensive appendix filled with a wide variety of mentoring exercises and sample contracts. Includes one-on-one activities for mentors and mentees and activities for enhancing the learning environment.

Shea, G. F. *Mentoring.* Los Altos, Calif.: Crisp, 1992.

Designed to help people identify and assess their own mentoring experiences, this workbook lays a solid foundation for developing successful mentor behaviors. It is filled with many exercises and practical how-to-do-it sections.

Conclusion

Mentoring is an age-old concept that readily incorporates the needs of today's rapidly changing society and professional demands. It is just one of many adult professional development strategies for fostering human and organizational potential. Tomorrow's technological world may change the formats in which of many of the resources described in this chapter are available. However, the most important resource, the bond developed between two caring human beings, will remain the same.

References

Bey, T. M., and Holmes, C. T. *Mentoring: Contemporary Principles and Issues.* Reston, Va.: Association of Teacher Educators, 1992.

Brockett, R. G. "Professional Association for Adult and Continuing Education." In S. B. Merriam and P. M. Cunningham (eds.), *Handbook of Adult and Continuing Education.* San Francisco: Jossey-Bass, 1989.

Brockett, R. G. "Strategies and Resources of Improving the Instructional Process." In M. W. Galbraith (ed.), *Facilitating Adult Learning: A Transactional Process.* Malabar, Fla.: Krieger, 1991.

Darkenwald, G. G., and Merriam, S. B. *Adult Education: Foundations of Practice.* New York: HarperCollins, 1982.

Hunt, D. M., and Michael, C. "Mentorship: A Career Training and Development Tool." *Academy of Management Review*, 1983, 8, 475–485.

Levinson, D., Darrow, C., Klein, E., Levinson, M., and McKee, B. *The Seasons of a Man's Life.* New York: Knopf, 1978.

Sheehy, G. *Passages: Predictable Crises of Adult Life.* New York: Dutton, 1976.

LINDA MARIE GOLIAN is serials department head for the Florida Atlantic University Libraries and assistant professor at Florida Atlantic University in Boca Raton.

An understanding of vexing issues and challenges is a foundation for advancing practice and research about the mentoring process.

Issues and Challenges Confronting Mentoring

Michael W. Galbraith, Norman H. Cohen

While this volume has discussed mentoring as it exists within formal or sponsored frameworks, it is important to recognize that mentoring exists informally as well. In informal as in formal mentoring, individuals find themselves engaged in a journey guided by someone they respect for his or her expertise, insights, wisdom, and vision. However, informal mentoring relationships seem to be the less understood of the two and the more difficult to explain in regard to their origins, to how and why the mentoring connection was made. All the same, both formal and informal mentoring are about the growth and development of people's personal, professional, and work lives. In this volume, the chapter authors have provided new insights concerning the process of mentoring within adult and continuing education practice and research. We believe that these insights offer better understanding of both sponsored and informal mentoring processes.

While the authors extend the knowledge base concerning mentoring, there are many issues that still confront mentors and mentees. The purpose of this chapter is to point out some of these issues and to describe how combined practice and research efforts are the most appropriate means of bringing about a better understanding of the mentoring process. In addition, the chapter concludes with some potential uses of mentoring in the adult and continuing education field.

Issues and Challenges

There are many challenges and issues concerning the enhancement of mentoring and its practice. Several of the primary ones are briefly described here.

Understanding the Misconceptions. One of the primary issues for adult and continuing education professionals to understand is that the current mentoring literature contains a number of misconceptions. Kram (1985) suggests several of these misconceptions.

The mentee is the primary beneficiary in the mentoring relationship. As the authors in Chapters Two through Six describe, mentoring relationships benefit the growth and development of the mentor, the organization, and the society as well.

A positive experience results for both the mentor and the mentee. Kram (1985, p. 196) writes that both mentors and mentees benefit in a developmental relationship; however, the relationship "is limited in its duration and value as individual needs and organizational circumstances change." Changing needs and circumstances may undermine the relationship and generate a lack of trust previously not experienced.

Mentoring relationships look the same in all settings. The mentoring relationship may vary depending upon the functions provided, program design, and level of commitment. The authors of Chapters One, Three, Four, and Six suggest that while common elements of mentoring exist, the setting in which mentoring takes place may influence the direction of the relationship.

Mentoring relationships are readily available to those who want them. Common sense and observation would suggest that neither sponsored nor informal mentoring has been a focus in the diverse settings and populations within adult and continuing education. All individuals who seek to have a mentoring relationship may not find such an opportunity.

Finding a mentor is the key to individual growth and professional advancement. Relying on one individual or mentor to provide all the essential elements for one's well-being and professional advancement is unwise. As Kram (1985, p. 200) writes, "Relationships with peers can also offer developmental functions, and individuals should develop a relationship constellation that consists of several relationships, each of which provides some career and/or psychosocial functions."

Definitional Dilemmas. Jacobi (1991, p. 506) states that "although many researchers have attempted to provide concise definitions of mentoring or mentors, definitional diversity continues to characterize the literature." Merriam (1983, p. 169) contends that "mentoring appears to mean one thing to developmental psychologists, another thing to business people, and a third thing to those in academic settings."

However, Golian and Galbraith (in press), after reviewing definitions from the literature in higher education, management and organizational behavior, psychology, library science, nursing, sociology, teacher education, counseling, and adult education, suggest that some common "themes" run through the definitions. They indicate that mentoring is a process within a contextual setting; involves a relationship of a more knowledgeable individual with a less experienced individual; provides professional networking, counseling, guiding, instructing, modeling, and sponsoring; is a developmental mechanism (personal, professional, and psychological); is a socialization and reciprocal relationship; and provides an identity transformation for both mentor and mentee.

While no universal definition of mentoring is accepted, these identified themes may provide a foundation for advancing a definition of mentoring that is appropriate for adult and continuing education practice and may also encourage further research.

Functions and Roles. In addressing definitional dilemmas, practitioners and researchers may also investigate and bring some resolution to the identification of the functions and roles within the mentoring process. Cohen's work (1995) and the insights in Chapters Two through Six of this volume can assist practitioners in advancing and identifying essential functions and roles. The functions and roles identified there may well be the primary ones we need to understand and may be useful in both sponsored and informal mentoring relationships.

Training of Mentors and Mentees. Hudson (1991) suggests that while many professionals provide mentoring services, most are not trained to do so. Cohen, in Chapter Two, renders a useful approach to assessing and preparing mentors with his Principles of Adult Mentoring Scale and its use as a training tool. Chapter Three, by Kerr, Schulze, and Woodward, and Chapter Four, by Johnson and Sullivan, provide excellent insights into the training of mentors and mentees through a well-designed orientation and follow-up activities. Golian, in Chapter Seven, provides superb advice for those who wish to conduct some independent study into the process of effective mentoring. If adult and continuing educators are going to be effective mentors and if adult learners are going to be effective mentees, then a deliberate effort must be made to acquire appropriate training. The benefits of mentoring suggested by Schulz in Chapter Five should be the result if proper training is secured.

Types of Research. Mentoring has been conducted using diverse research designs (Jacobi, 1991). Adult and continuing education practitioners and researchers have much to contribute to the understanding of mentoring through quantitative quasi-experimental research and ethnographic and qualitative methods. The practitioner-as-researcher process should be encouraged. It will be through this method that the mentoring relationship will gain greater understanding, meaning, and focus. Jacobi (1991, p. 521) states that mentoring research "needs valid and reliable measurement instruments." Cohen, in Chapter Two, provides for the reader a valid and reliable instrument whose use can encourage further research.

In addition, research is needed concerning the mentoring relationship as it relates to issues of gender, race, diversity, academic success, age, technology use, contextual settings, effectiveness, career advancement, lifelong learning, program design and operations, benefits, personal growth and development, evaluation, ethics, theory building, and so forth. Many intriguing research designs and topics warrant further investigation to advance our knowledge base about mentoring.

Potential Uses

It has been suggested throughout this volume that mentoring is about growth and development within an individual's personal, professional, social, and psychological worlds. It is about transition, identity, and active movement in the hopes of reaching one's highest potential and capabilities. Given the diverse settings in which adult and continuing education takes place, and considering the multiple purposes of the field (personal development, promotion of productivity, social change, support and maintenance of the good social order) (Beder, 1989), mentoring holds great potential for adult learners, organizations, and communities.

The various chapters in this volume detail some of these possibilities associated with mentoring. Perhaps the greatest potential for mentoring is in the development of lifelong learning opportunities within the community and in the improvement of instruction. These are areas of inquiry that need more attention.

Extending Lifelong Learning Opportunities. In a commissioned paper, Galbraith (1995) suggests that everyone has some expertise in something and that someone in the community probably is seeking an opportunity to acquire knowledge about that same thing. The problem is, how can those who have the knowledge and those who seek it connect? Through the development of community-based mentoring programs, resource lists, and the use of technology, these mentoring relationships could be developed. Extending lifelong learning opportunities through community-based organizations such as businesses and industries, religious institutions, social and fraternal groups, schools, colleges, universities, self-help groups, health-related and human service agencies, senior citizen centers, farmer institutes, libraries, museums, labor unions, and so forth is the key to the success and development of a learning society. From this perspective, everyone is capable of being a teacher (mentor) *and* a learner (mentee). Through the use of technology, electronic mentoring is now available as well. This is an area that holds much promise for the development of lifelong learners in urban and rural communities. It may result in extended learning opportunities offered not just at the local level but worldwide.

Improvement of Instruction. If we can understand what good mentoring functions and roles are, then we can translate them into what good instruction should be about. In Chapter Two, Cohen suggests that mentoring functions include building a relationship, providing information, being facilitative, being challenging, serving as a role model, and providing a vision. These same functions, although under different names at times, are discussed in the adult and continuing education literature on good instruction (see, for example, Brookfield, 1990; Daloz, 1986; Galbraith, 1991; Hiemstra and Sisco, 1990). If we are concerned with creating a conducive climate for learning and for designing and developing useful syllabi and materials, encouraging learners to be critically and reflectively thoughtful, challenging learners to think and act differently, stimulating professionals to serve as role models in authentic and credible ways, and creating a vision for what could be in relation to mentees' personal and professional potential, then good mentoring has much to offer those of us interested in being skillful instructors for adult learners. Regardless of what is taught or where it takes place, mentoring functions can enhance our instructional process.

Conclusion

Galbraith and Zelenak (1991, p. 126) suggest that mentoring is "a powerful emotional, and passionate interaction whereby the mentor and protégé experience personal, professional, and intellectual growth and development." Their definition focuses on the possibilities of mentoring relationships and the opportunities for new experiences in uncharted territory. Adult learners, organizations, and communities can realize the extension of lifelong learning opportunities, growth, and development through sponsored and informal mentoring. And it will be through informed adult and continuing practitioners and researchers working in a collaborative manner that the knowledge base, practice, and research related to mentoring will be advanced.

References

Beder, H. "Purposes and Philosophies of Adult Education." In S. B. Merriam and P. M. Cunningham (eds.), Handbook of Adult and Continuing Education. San Francisco: Jossey-Bass, 1989.

Brookfield, S. D. The Skillful Teacher: On Technique, Trust, and Responsiveness in the Classroom. San Francisco: Jossey-Bass, 1990.

Cohen, N. H. Mentoring Adult Learners: A Guide for Educators and Trainers. Malabar, Fla.: Krieger, 1995.

Daloz, L. A. Effective Teaching and Mentoring: Realizing the Transformational Power of Adult Learning Experiences. San Francisco: Jossey-Bass, 1986.

Galbraith, M. W. (ed.). Facilitating Adult Learning: A Transactional Process. Malabar, Fla.: Krieger, 1991.

Galbraith, M. W. "Community-Based Organizations and the Delivery of Lifelong Learning Opportunities." Paper presented to the National Institute on Postsecondary Education, Libraries, and Lifelong Learning, Washington, D.C., Apr. 12, 1995.

Galbraith, M. W., and Zelenak, B. S. "Adult Learning Methods and Techniques." In M. W. Galbraith (ed.), Facilitating Adult Learning: A Transactional Process. Malabar, Fla.: Krieger, 1991.

Golian, L. M., and Galbraith, M. W. "Creating Effective Mentoring Programs for Professional Library Development." Advances in Library Administration and Organization, in press.

Hiemstra, R., and Sisco, B. Individualizing Instruction: Making Learning Personal, Empowering, and Successful. San Francisco: Jossey-Bass, 1990.

Hudson, F. M. The Adult Years: Mastering the Art of Self-Renewal. San Francisco: Jossey-Bass, 1991.

Jacobi, M. "Mentoring and Undergraduate Academic Success: A Literature Review." Review of Educational Research, 1991, 61 (4), 505–532.

Kram, K. E. Mentoring at Work: Developmental Relationships in Organizational Life. Glenview, Ill.: Scott, Foresman, 1985.

Merriam, S. B. "Mentors and Protégés: A Critical Review of the Literature." Adult Education Quarterly, 1983, 33 (3), 161–173.

MICHAEL W. GALBRAITH is professor of adult education in the Department of Educational Leadership at Florida Atlantic University in Boca Raton.

NORMAN H. COHEN is associate professor of English at the Community College of Philadelphia.

INDEX

ORDERING INFORMATION

NEW DIRECTIONS FOR ADULT AND CONTINUING EDUCATION is a series of paperback books that explores issues of common interest to instructors, administrators, counselors, and policy makers in a broad range of adult and continuing education settings—such as colleges and universities, extension programs, businesses, the military, prisons, libraries, and museums. Books in the series are published quarterly in Spring, Summer, Fall, and Winter and are available for purchase by subscription and individually.

SUBSCRIPTIONS for 1995 cost $48.00 for individuals (a savings of 25 percent over single-copy prices) and $64.00 for institutions, agencies, and libraries. Please do not send institutional checks for personal subscriptions. Standing orders are accepted. (For subscriptions outside of North America, add $7.00 for shipping via surface mail or $25.00 for air mail. Orders *must be prepaid* in U.S. dollars by check drawn on a U.S. bank or charged to VISA, MasterCard, or American Express.)

SINGLE COPIES cost $19.00 plus shipping (see below) when payment accompanies order. California, New Jersey, New York, and Washington, D.C., residents please include appropriate sales tax. Canadian residents add GST and any local taxes. Billed orders will be charged shipping and handling. No billed shipments to post office boxes. (Orders from outside North America *must be prepaid* in U.S. dollars by check drawn on a U.S. bank or charged to VISA, MasterCard, or American Express.)

SHIPPING (SINGLE COPIES ONLY): one issue, add $3.50; two issues, add $4.50; three issues, add $5.50; four to five issues, add $6.50; six to seven issues, add $7.50; eight or more issues, add $8.50.

DISCOUNTS FOR QUANTITY ORDERS are available. Please write to the address below for information.

ALL ORDERS must include either the name of an individual or an official purchase order number. Please submit your order as follows:
 Subscriptions: specify series and year subscription is to begin
 Single copies: include individual title code (such as ACE 59)

MAIL ALL ORDERS TO:
 Jossey-Bass Publishers
 350 Sansome Street
 San Francisco, California 94104-1342

FOR SUBSCRIPTION SALES OUTSIDE OF THE UNITED STATES, contact any international subscription agency or Jossey-Bass directly.